What a
GOOD EATER!

BABY & TODDLER RECIPES WITH HEALTHY HERBS &
SPICES TO ADD FLAVOR & BROADEN YOUR BABY'S PALATE

ALESSANDRA MACALUSO & AMY GODIWALLA

CONTENTS

Cover designed by Alessandra Macaluso, Amy Godiwalla and Devin Gamble;
photographed by Shaun Kruse
Photography by Shaun Kruse
Photo editing by Devin Gamble
Food Styling by Alessandra Macaluso and Amy Godiwalla
Interior page layouts designed by Devin Gamble

DEDICATION

This book is for my sweet children, Landon and Armin. I love you and am so proud of you in every way.

-Amy

For Penelope and Ciro, for Greg, and for all of the family who have inspired me and led me on this journey.

-Alessandra

We also dedicate this book to every parent and caregiver who feeds their little ones with love. We hope our recipes inspire you and fill your homes with enticing aromas, inevitable spills, and the sounds of baby giggles and satisfied burps.

ACKNOWLEDGMENTS

We wish to thank all of the clinical experts we consulted for this cookbook. Their knowledge and expertise helped us incorporate nutritious recipes and relevant baby-related details that help make our book informative, nutritious, and safe. Among them, we'd like to say a special thank you to both Dr. Elissa Levine, pediatrician, and Registered Dietician JuliSu DiMucci-Ward, who went above and beyond with their guidance and thoughtful information. Please visit "Professional Biographies of Doctors and Specialists" for full information on those we've consulted throughout our journey.

Thank you to our wonderful photographer, Shaun Kruse, for beautifully capturing our recipes in the photographs in the book. Your pictures speak a thousand words.

We extend our deepest gratitude to the many recipe testers across the nation who followed our recipes, tried them on their own children and families, and provided us with detailed feedback and suggestions for improvement.

We'd also like to say a special thank you to the other professionals who helped us, guided us, and provided us their expertise, among them Devin Gamble, for the beautiful book design and photo editing, Michelle Stalnaker, for her legal advice and support, and Ann Thrash, for her editing services.

Lastly, and most importantly, this book wouldn't exist without our children. Penelope, Ciro, Landon, and Armin, you have been the greatest sports through our two-year journey writing this book and developing recipes. You have tasted many recipes and told us, very bluntly, whether or not they were acceptable. Thank you for humoring us and for becoming the fantastic, open-minded, well-rounded eaters you are today. We love you!

CO-AUTHOR ALESSANDRA'S PERSONAL ACKNOWLEDGMENTS:

Thank you to my children, Penelope and Ciro, for providing endless inspiration and the will to create this book. To my husband, Greg, for always believing in me and for helping corral the kids while I worked. To my parents, for always being interested and encouraging and for providing me with the invaluable foundation of a solid work ethic. I love you all so very much.

To my grandparents on both sides, and the many others who have come before me and shown me their love through the meals they've prepared, thank you today and always for being an inspiration. Thank you to my co-author, Amy, for agreeing to create this book with me and for being so committed and fun to work with, and to her husband, Shaun, for taking all of these stunning photographs.

CO-AUTHOR AMY'S PERSONAL ACKNOWLEDGMENTS:

Thank you to my husband, Shaun, for taking the spectacular photographs in this cookbook. You have maintained high standards throughout our project, and I am so pleased your photographs will live in our book. I am grateful you have given me the opportunity to work on something that fills my heart with joy—something that makes me truly happy. I love you.

Thank you, Mom, for being a fabulous cook and for supporting me with your contagious enthusiasm during the making of this book. You are my number one fan. To my beloved father: I have thought of you and missed you on countless occasions while working with various ingredients and inventing recipes. You made me a believer in the importance of herbs, spices, and maintaining an overall healthy diet. To my grandmother: You took tremendous care to feed us well when we were children. I had no idea what an impact you would have on me one day. And thank you to my co-author, Alessandra (Ali). You have accompanied me on a project that I am overjoyed and passionate about—a creation that was an absolute blast in the making!

DISCLAIMER

This book has been created and written by two mothers based on their personal experiences and recipes to assist other parents with the introduction of solid foods to their babies. The information provided, while thoroughly researched and backed with personal and professional experience, is presented for educational purposes only. The recipes in this book are intended for healthy children. If you are dealing with any medical issues, such as allergies, colic, reflux, etc., we strongly encourage you to consult your child's pediatrician for guidance. This book is not intended to replace professional medical advice. *Always consult a medical professional before introducing new foods and ingredients to your baby.*

DIETARY AND ALLERGEN RESTRICTIONS: Our recipes do not and will not cater to specific allergy or dietary restrictions. The recipes and suggested ingredients may not be suitable for consumption or use by vegans, vegetarians, or those with religious, dietary, or use restrictions, as they may contain various animal products, including, but not limited to, butter, eggs, honey, lard, meat by-products and derivatives, milk, tallow, etc. Additionally, the recipes and suggested ingredients may not be suitable for consumption or use by those with allergy concerns, as they may contain ingredients that contain or have come in contact with one or more of the following ingredients, any one of which can produce an allergic or other medical reaction:

1. Wheat and its derivatives
2. Gluten and its derivatives
3. Corn and its derivatives
4. Soybeans and their derivatives
5. Eggs (whole, whites, and/or yolks)
6. Milk and milk products/derivatives
7. Fish
8. Shellfish
9. Tree nuts and their derivatives
10. Peanuts and their derivatives
11. Tree nut oils and their derivatives
12. Peanut oil and their derivatives
13. Tree nut extracts
14. Strawberry
15. Natural dyes
16. Natural flavorings
17. Artificial dyes
18. Artificial flavorings
19. Sugar
20. Artificial sweeteners
21. Other allergens not listed

All product and service references and suggestions are provided for informational purposes only. Accordingly, no part of this book is intended to suggest or represent endorsements or sponsorships. The authors and publishers offer no guarantees in accordance with the information provided and disclaim all liability in connection with its use. Similarities to actual persons other than those expressly identified are coincidental.

Additionally, up-to-date resources available from government agencies such as the U.S. Food and Drug Administration (www.fda.gov), the American Heart Association (http://www.heart.org), and the United States Department of Agriculture (www.usda.gov) may be very helpful.

INTRODUCTION

In the early days with our babies, we remember looking at them and thinking: Dear Lord, they have to eat *real food* one day? Life with an infant on merely a liquid diet seemed hard enough! Real food felt like it was eons away and too overwhelming to even consider at the time. But as we neared the 6 month milestone and life with a baby slowly became more manageable, we began to feel both ready and excited to introduce solid foods.

But where to start?

At our doctor appointments, we were sent home with a one-sheeter on "baby's first foods" explaining...well, hardly anything helpful. We unfortunately left those appointments with more questions than we had going in.

We've seen the photos of the adorable baby, food smeared all over her smiling face, opening wide for Mama as the miniature spoon is airplaned into her mouth. But once it's time for you to be the mama or papa bird to your own little one, you'll want to know many things:

- *What exactly is on the spoon?*
- *How much do I feed my baby, and how many times per day?*
- *What should his first food even be?*
- *Is it safe to feed him our family's favorite foods?*
- *Which foods are healthiest?*
- *How can I safely add flavors?*
- *Can I use herbs and spices, and if so, how much?*

It was these questions, coupled with our intentions to feed our babies wholesome, healthful, flavorful foods, that led us on our journey to create this book. A journey filled with messy kitchens, satisfied tummies, enticing aromas, freezers chock-full of healthy, ready-to-go meals, and plenty of food tossed over the side of high chairs. You'll be happy to know that we picked up on their not-so-subtle signs!

What a Good Eater! is a cookbook filled with nutritious recipes for babies and toddlers; a guide for parents to confidently feed their babies and toddlers wholesome, healthy, age-appropriate foods that help promote a diverse palate

right from the get-go. We are two moms who believe that introducing flavorful foods using healthy herbs and spices encourages exploration and openness, minimizes picky eating habits, and sets the stage—and table—for positive future family meal experiences.

Dear Lord, they have to eat real food one day?

WHY HOMEMADE BABY FOOD?

Chances are, if you're holding this book, you are already interested in the idea of preparing fresh, homemade foods for your little one. Or, your mother-in-law gave it to you for your baby shower, and you're sweating at the thought of even attempting to prepare fresh foods for your baby! Either way, the experience that comes from turning raw, whole ingredients into literally weeks' worth of food for your baby is a wonderful thing—and when we're talking about baby food, you would be surprised at how very simple it can be! Here are just a few of our favorite reasons for preparing your baby's foods:

- *You'll be amazed at how much food even one simple ingredient can produce.*
- *It's easier than you think.*
- *You'll have a freezer full of nutritious options for meals needed on the fly.*
- *It's less expensive than buying prepackaged foods.*
- *It can introduce you to flavors, herbs, and spices that you never knew you or your family would like.*
- *Preparing a meal, even just once or twice per week, can have a healthful impact on your entire family.*
- *It can awaken your love for cooking.*
- *It can light a creative, adventurous spark in your child.*

We want to stress that you do not need to be a seasoned cook to follow our recipes (although if you already love to cook, that is great!). You'll be happy to know that our recipes are designed for simplicity. We wanted our book to be approachable for all parents, even those who cook very little, if at all, and who may want to start now.

And, when you think about it, if you are getting ready to feed your little one his first foods, what better time and what better motivation to begin preparing home-cooked meals for yourself and the rest of your family?

We've combined the advice and knowledge of many pediatricians, nutritionists, dieticians, and specialists while crafting our recipes to ensure that they are safe, age appropriate, and well rounded for babies. These are the meals we feed to our own children time and again—our go-to recipes from our babies' first bites all the way through to what we eat as a family today. We hope you will do the same for your babies and families too.

WHY HERBS AND SPICES?

When we first dove into this project, the question was, "Why herbs and spices?" but it quickly became, "Why not?" In looking at other countries and cultures, herbs and spices are introduced to a baby's diet straight from the get-go, and there was no reason we couldn't do the same thing—so long as we did so gently, and with respect for our babies' palates.

It's easy to think that a clove of garlic or smidge of herbs here and there couldn't possibly have a significant impact on the overall health of your child and your family. But we have learned that it absolutely can! You might wonder: How can that small amount of herbs and spices help my baby? Are there any real benefits to using them? Our answer is a resounding *yes*. Not only do they make baby food (and adult food!) more palatable and interesting, but they also can provide health benefits—and they are very easy to cook with.

When we zoom out and look at these small changes as a whole, we can begin to see how they work together and act as the canvas for our child's overall health. Naturopathic Doctor Stephanie Mottola put it best:

" *Introducing children to these varying tastes at a young age can help expand their palate for years to come and help encourage them to be more adventurous eaters. This could make for ultimately healthier eaters in the long run. Good nutrition can prevent the need for pharmaceutical medicine, so this is no small thing!*

Food is our greatest medicine, and herbs and spices are food. They provide the body with micronutrients needed to fuel the activity of every cell in our body, antioxidants to protect each cell and organ that make us healthy and strong, along with many other, previously unnamed compounds being "discovered" daily that help our organs to function healthfully. I think they also help introduce our children to what real, earth-given food tastes like and help to bring delicious flavor to our food, encouraging healthy eating of whole, unprocessed foods. Generally speaking, food that is healthy and safe for an adult is healthy and safe for a baby, in small amounts. "

The more we thought about it, the more it made sense: How could we offer first foods to our babies that were bland, lacking in flavor, and repetitive—and then expect them to become good, well-rounded eaters later on? The experts we consulted agreed: starting off with flavors and diverse food options from the earliest stages of eating laid the groundwork for better eaters later on.

We think you'll find, as we did, that using herbs and spices is easy and helps introduce your child to a world of flavor beyond bland foods. And it doesn't hurt that food has a tremendous power to heal, as well as support overall health. (For a full list of the herbs and spices we use in our recipes, as well as their benefits, visit our "Glossary of Herbs and Spices.")

OUR "DIETS"

As we're sure you've seen, there are tons of "diets" out there, and we've seen them for babies too. Each of them of course claims to be the "healthiest" option.

We don't buy in to these labels. Our philosophy is that while there might be healthy aspects of each of these diets, a well-rounded approach to eating is best. Our cookbook does not fit into a particular "diet" except for what we consider to be a healthy one. We feel that it is more important to focus on the *quality* of our ingredients, such as purchasing organic when possible, cooking with nutritional and flavorful ingredients, choosing grass-fed meats (if the recipe calls for meat), sourcing locally when we are able, and staying away from processed foods. Our recipes place great emphasis on foods in their most natural form.

In this book you'll find excellent recipes that fall into

many different categories—Mediterranean style, ethnic, vegetarian, vegan, savory meat and fish recipes, and fun twists on American fan favorites, to name a few—all crafted with a focus on nutrition, ease of preparation, and quality. Many of them will yield large quantities, providing plenty to freeze for later, because not many of us busy parents can cook every day! We know we can't!

You'll also notice that for most of the recipes in our book you will not find specific serving amounts. Instead, we provide the amount of food the recipe will yield. The reason for this is because each child varies in their appetites, and many of our meals are family friendly.

Therefore, serving sizes will vary greatly since both adults and babies are eating the same foods in different quantities. We do offer estimated serving sizes as a guideline in the Sample Food Schedules that appear at the start of each recipe section.

SOMETHING FOR EVERYONE

This book was made for little eaters, as you can see from our age-appropriate recipes, but our recipes were also crafted with the whole family in mind. You will find that many of them are family friendly, and this is both to encourage family meals and to relieve parents from having to cook twice or serve different meals to different family members.

This book also serves as an excellent invitation for older toddlers and young children to learn about herbs and spices and to pique their culinary curiosity. How inter-

esting for them to learn they can sweeten their food with cinnamon, rather than sugar! How incredible to find they can add flavor with parsley, rather than salt? How exciting for them to discover that they can take control of their meals! You never know what a love of food can spark in the imagination of little ones, and you're helping them understand that there are many different ways to prepare foods and add flavors. A healthy relationship with food is important, and it's never too early to begin.

As parents and caregivers, we don't need to cook anything fancy or be five-star chefs to get the most out of this book. We know it is hard to prepare anything from scratch these days. But some of our best memories are of being in the kitchen with our parents or grandparents, hearing the stories they told while preparing us fresh meals, how our full tummies felt warm and loved—and how much we think of them today.

We certainly don't have, and don't pretend to have, obedient little eaters who will feast upon anything we prepare for them without fuss or protest. After all, they are toddlers now, and they have plenty of opinions! But we can say with confidence that they do eat very well, enjoy a nutritious diet, and are open to trying new things—and we credit much of this to our recipes and our commitment to offering a variety of flavors, textures, and ingredients. We also discovered several recipes that quickly became favorites for our families, providing us endless options at mealtimes and freezers filled with ready-to-go meals on the fly.

Whether you are a regular foodie and novice cook with plans to prepare the majority of your family's meals, a super busy parent with limited time to cook, a newbie to cooking who would like a beautiful reference book with great recipes to try, or a family member looking for a great gift for a mom-to-be, we believe there is something for everyone inside these pages. We hope you enjoy it as much as we enjoyed creating it. If you'd like to keep up with our project and stay up-to-date with new recipes, blog posts, and more, visit: http://whatagoodeater.com.

AUTHOR BIOGRAPHIES:

Amy Godiwalla

Amy Godiwalla was born and raised in a Parsi (Persian-Indian) family in Houston, Texas. Amy's grandmother, a renowned caterer in India, cooked for many special guests during her lifetime, including government officials, diplomats, and even the queen of England. Her grandmother later emigrated from India to the United States to live with Amy's family, where she prepared delicious meals daily. Amy's mother, a talented cook herself, frequently cooked foods from different countries in 30 minutes or less. Amy's exposure to different foods at an impressionable age was welcome and customary.

After graduating from the University of Texas at Austin, Amy studied foreign language and culture in Florence, Italy, and Seville, Spain. She returned to the United States and excelled in the corporate world, holding various sales and marketing positions and winning numerous awards at Fortune 500 companies. After 14 successful years in corporate America, Amy proudly accepted a new promotion: full-time caregiver to her two sons, Landon and Armin! She began feeding Landon homemade baby food with herbs and spices, which sparked the inspiration and collaboration for *What a Good Eater!*

Amy and her husband, Shaun, live in Denver, Colorado, with their two little boys. When Amy is not feeding little mouths or inventing recipes, she enjoys hiking, yoga, snowboarding, cooking, entertaining, traveling to the mountains, sipping hot chocolate at ski resorts, and wine tasting.

Before having my first child, I researched how to minimize picky eating habits in children. I discovered that the subject fascinated me! My research confirmed my intuition: exposing children to a variety of foods, flavors, and textures at a very young age is imperative. I hope to raise children who enjoy a variety of cuisines and flavors, welcoming them with enthusiasm and curiosity. I would be delighted and honored if I can help other parents also achieve this goal.

Alessandra Macaluso

Alessandra (Ali) Macaluso is the author of *The Real-Deal Bridal Bible*, the voice behind her lifestyle blog, *PunkWife*, and regular contributor to *The Huffington Post* and *Scary Mommy*. Her work has appeared in several other media publications, which can all be found on her author site, www.alessandramacaluso.com.

Alessandra graduated from Pace University with a B.A. in English and Communications. She lives in Charlotte, NC with her husband Greg, their two small children, Penelope and Ciro, and a 25 lb. cat named Marcus who believes he is a dog.

Her inspiration behind *What a Good Eater!* began with her desire to feed her daughter healthy meals on-the-fly. A busy mom, like many of us, Ali wanted an approachable way to introduce great flavors to her daughter beginning with the first bites. Her collaboration for this project is the delicious result. She has always enjoyed cooking and entertaining, and has forever been intrigued and amazed by the healing powers of herbs and spices. She is inspired by the cooking styles of both of her grandmothers: her father's mother, a strong Italian woman who lived for cooking savory meals and would even make her own pasta, and her mother's mother, equally strong, who considers herself a "lousy cook" but taught Ali that you only need to learn to "make one good dish", a feat which she accomplished through her addictive eggplant parmesan.

" I'm a first-generation Italian with a passion for food, and a desire to keep things simple. I found that a direct result of feeding our daughter no-fuss, flavorful meals was a beneficial change in our diets as well. My favorite recipes in our book are the ones designed for the whole family to enjoy. "

OUR STORY

There are many reasons why we set out to create this book, ranging from the friendship we've developed between our families, going all the way back to our roots as individuals. We'd like to take a moment to share that story with you. Because this project is more than just a book; it's actually a lifetime in the making, and a true labor of love.

ALESSANDRA (ALI'S) STORY

I brought my daughter, Penelope, over to Amy's house one day when the babies were small. Amy's son Landon is 3 months older than Penelope (he was 8-months-old at the time) and had already started eating solid foods. Amy was spoon-feeding him a bright orange puree with specs of green in it, and whatever it was, he was *wolfing it down* like a champ!

> *"What is he eating?"* I asked.

> *"Butternut squash, with rosemary and sage!"* Amy said.

> I sat there, baffled for a minute. *"Babies can eat herbs at this age?"*

> *"Yes, they can!"* Amy responded confidently.

I went home that night and my mind began racing. I am a foodie at heart, and a first-generation Italian, meaning that I come from a whole line of people who also care a great deal about food.

I thought of my nonna Tina, my father's mother, who would create a feast from her tiny kitchen in their apartment in the Bronx, where we'd eat until we felt like we'd burst, and all the while she was serving us more, insisting, "Mangia, mangia!" ("Eat, eat!"). Food was love.

I thought of my grandmother, my mother's mother, who was the first to admit she was a "lousy cook," but who perfected an eggplant Parmesan that has yet to be surpassed and who used to make my day with her English muffin pizzas. She taught me one of the most important pieces of culinary advice: *you don't have to know how to cook a lot of things, but if you learn how to cook just a handful of things well, and with love, you've succeeded as a chef.*

I think of my own mother, who, somewhere in between raising five children and working outside of the home, still grew a family garden on the side of our house. I remember as a child declaring tomatoes "disgusting!" until the time I had fresh-picked, home-grown chunks of tomatoes straight from the vine, tossed in olive oil and oregano. It blew my mind that those tomatoes were still growing only minutes before we ate them. Suddenly, from that point on, they were *delicious*.

I had always considered myself a fairly healthy eater, but once I became pregnant, food took on a whole new meaning. It suddenly became a priority for me because it was no longer just myself I was eating healthily for—I was now responsible for our baby's health as well.

I knew I wanted to prepare Penelope's food when her time came to start eating, and I knew that I didn't want it to be bland. I love food too much, and I wanted my daughter to love it too! We keep a small garden at home, where we grow herbs and whatever fresh food we can, so this seemed a natural step.

But my mind was racing from a nutritional standpoint as well. We know that herbs and spices are beneficial to adults and that they enhance the flavor profiles of our foods tremendously. Surely they had to be beneficial for babies too?

I knew Amy shared my love for food, as well as nutritious ingredients. She loved experimenting with new recipes, and I had been creating and sharing recipes on my personal website for many years already. We are busy moms, so practicality is always a top priority. We were both hard workers who had recently left our jobs to become hardworking, full-time caregivers to our babies, and we were now embarking on this journey in feeding them. Suddenly, a light bulb went on in my head!

I went back to Amy's the following week with a proposition: Would she like to collaborate on a cookbook for babies and toddlers, using delicious flavors, herbs, and spices? I thought for a moment she might think I was a bit crazy, but when I was met with an enthusiastic and resounding "*Yes!*" I knew she was just as excited about this idea as I was.

AMY'S STORY

I vividly remember the first time I fed my son solid foods. I prepared my own homemade puree in the blender, placed Landon in a bouncy chair on the kitchen floor, spoon-fed him a few bites, and had my husband capture every moment on video! I felt alive and energized by this milestone—even more so than the first time he crawled or walked. Perhaps my enthusiasm stemmed from my passion for cooking, nutrition, and eating!

I felt confident about what I wanted to feed my son, even though my resume displayed zero prior experience. Much of my confidence came from the vast research I did on how to introduce solid foods and prevent picky eating habits in children. I also trusted my own intuition. Many of the foods I fed my son during his early years were foods that my husband and I enjoyed before we had children. Dishes such as roasted brussels sprouts with fresh thyme and butternut squash with rosemary and sage were perfect side vegetables for our dinner. My goal was to have my kids eat the same foods my husband and I ate, *so why not start as soon as possible?* I wanted to expose my children to various flavors and foods *as soon as it was safe to do so.*

My husband's hobby is gardening. On a regular basis, we grew food in the garden, cooked healthy meals, and enjoyed romantic, candlelit dinners at home prior to having kids. We didn't want these traditions to drastically change after kids. Once the kids came along, our candles and matches flew right out the window, but luckily our passion for eating healthy meals did not!

I had the privilege of growing up in a Parsi (Persian-Indian) household. Food was a critical part of our family life and a primary expression of love. My three sisters and I were fortunate to grow up with our Parsi, live-in grandmother. She was a well-known caterer in India, and she emigrated to the United States to live with my parents in the late 1970s. At the time, I had no idea what an influence my grandmother would have on me one day. Like her, I now take intense pleasure from watching my kids devour food I have lovingly prepared for them.

Growing up, my parents and grandmother followed somewhat of a naturopathic approach to treating illnesses. Eastern medicine, including the use of herbs, spices, and foods, was often "prescribed" by my parents. If that did not work, we would resort to traditional Western medicine. My father and grandmother were the family's main prescribers of these herbal remedies.

Congested?

"*Drink warm milk with turmeric!*" my father would advise in a heavy, British-Indian accent. "*The turmeric will help break up the mucus and knock it out!*"

Have a sore throat?

"*Take hot water, brandy, and honey before you go to bed. Use local farmer's honey. It's the best!*" he'd explain.

"*What's the honey for?*" I'd ask.

"*The honey helps coat your throat and makes it feel nice. The hot water helps the honey mix well.*"

"*And the brandy? What medicinal purpose does that serve?*" I'd ask.

At first, I got no response, so I asked the question again.

"*The brandy? Well, that's just to help you sleep well,*" he admitted softly.

Nauseous? No problem!

"*Take lavang (clove)!*" my Parsi grandmother would recommend. She'd excitedly run upstairs to her bedroom, open her top dresser drawer, and pull a single clove out of a McCormick's spice bottle.

"Suck on this slowly," she'd say. I'd be left standing there in awe, uncertain of what to do with the bizarre-looking spice that was shaped like a small, single-stem rose.

Constipated?

"Take isabgol (psyllium husk) mixed with a little orange juice!" my mom would exclaim. *"It makes your bowel movements smoooth as silk!"* She had an American accent that sounded so natural, you'd never know she was actually born in Bombay.

As a child, all of these herbal remedies sounded more superstitious than medicinal. But over the years, I grew to believe that foods, herbs, and spices can play a big role in our overall health. I believe that in some instances, they may even aid certain ailments.

In October 2013, Alessandra approached me about working on a baby food cookbook that featured the use of herbs and spices. To say I was excited is a gross understatement—I was thrilled! Two months later, my husband, Landon, and I boarded a plane to Houston. We were on our way to spend Christmas and New Year's at my parents' house. The day after we arrived, my father unexpectedly suffered a heart attack. Later that week, we attended his funeral. I never imagined that would be the last time my father would see Landon. Due to geography, my father had met our son only twice: once when Landon was 2-months-old and then a second time at 8-months-old, the day before my father passed away. I had exactly two photographs of them together.

After my visit to Houston, I grappled with some difficult decisions. *Would I be in a healthy mind-set to work on this cookbook? Could I fully focus and commit to this project?* Somewhere along the way, the answer to these questions became clear. My parents are the reason I am feeding my kids the way I'm feeding them. Creating this cookbook would be an opportunity to work on something I love, something I am doing with my children anyway, and, on many levels, it would help me keep memories of my dad alive. He was the one who made me a believer in the importance and benefits of herbs and spices in the first place.

During the many late nights I stood in my kitchen inventing recipes for this cookbook, I'd hold different foods, herbs, and spices in my hand and hear my dad's voice in my head. His voice was telling me the same things he told me over and over when he was alive:

> *"Amy, garlic is very good for the immune system, nutmeg is good for digestion, cardamom is good for heartburn, lime is good for dehydration…"*

OUR JOURNEY BEGINS

Before we knew it, our get-togethers with our babies turned into sessions filled with cooking, recipe testing, and writing, peppered with feeding our babies and planned (and failed) attempts at nap synchronization. As anyone with a baby or toddler knows, taking care of babies is hard work! But the good part was that we had built-in recipe testers right there with us. Many times we would meet at night after our babies were in bed to work on marketing, management of our project, and business details, which we still do today.

When it came to cooking styles and flavors, we drew upon our own ethnic backgrounds and family favorites (Italian and Indian), as well as favorite tastes from around the world and classic American favorites too. We also interviewed and consulted with pediatricians, dieticians, specialists, and other experts when crafting our recipes to ensure we were creating the most nutritious food combinations and using the healthiest ingredients, all while being respectful to our little ones' sensitive palates. And, perhaps the most important part of our journey, we tapped our growing network of moms and dads who are also raising and feeding little ones and who willingly took our recipes for test drives and gave us real feedback and suggestions along the way. We knew we did not want to cook separate meals for our children, so we also made sure that many of our recipes could be enjoyed by the entire family, too.

The result of all the above is the beautiful book in your hands: one we know is filled with not just recipes and flavors, but also thoughtfulness, gentle encouragement, and lots and lots of love.

SAMPLE FOOD SCHEDULE
FOR 6-MONTH-OLD BABY

The following feeding schedule is a sample of what one mom feeds her 6-month-old baby. This is simply one example that is intended to act as a guide only. All babies have different feeding times and eat different quantities. We recommend that you consult your pediatrician with any questions or concerns with regards to feeding your baby.

If a food name is italicized, that means you'll find the recipe in this book.

7:00 A.M. (BREAKFAST):	8 ounces breast milk or formula
11:00 A.M. (LUNCH):	2–3 tablespoons solid foods, such as *Only Oats, Simple Sweet Potatoes,* or *Clean Carrots* 6 ounces breast milk or formula
2:30 P.M. (SNACK):	2–3 tablespoons solid foods, such as *Velvety Prunes* or *Bare Pear* 6 ounces breast milk or formula
6:00 P.M. (DINNER):	8 ounces breast milk or formula

Tip: Try feeding your baby a "rainbow" of solid foods throughout the day so that she gets a variety of nutrition. For example, if you serve something orange for lunch, try serving something green, yellow, or red for a different meal.

6 MONTHS PLUS:
BABY'S FIRST FOODS

In this chapter we focus on healthy, powerhouse foods that produce a beautiful array of colors—deep purples, vibrant greens, gorgeous oranges—you'll have a hard time believing they are made from single ingredients!

We've selected these first foods for baby because they are flavorful and nutritious, but also because they are the "building blocks" upon which we base future recipes. This stage is a fun one too, because you get to see the adorable (and often funny!) faces your baby makes when she explores different flavors for the very first time. Many of our recipes in this section will yield large quantities (so you'll have plenty to freeze for future meals) and we include tips on how to make the leftovers into an adult snack or side dish.

Beginning with colorful foods, right from the early stages of eating, can offer your baby an excellent start with her health. "Colorful fruits and vegetables are high in antioxidants. Antioxidants protect our cells and every tissue in our body from damage and can help relieve symptoms of allergies and congestion," explains Naturopathic Doctor Stephanie Mottola.

The main points to remember during this stage are:

- BE SURE BABY IS READY TO EAT SOLID FOODS. Start her off right and make sure she is indeed ready to enjoy foods other than breast milk or formula. (See our "Frequently Asked Questions and Helpful Information" chapter for signs your baby is ready to start solids.)
- START SLOW. You can begin by feeding just one meal of solid food per day.
- THINK SMALL. Just a tablespoon, or even a teaspoon, will usually do the trick at first. Babies have little tummies! We suggest freezing leftovers in an ice cube tray or in small (two or four ounces) airtight containers. In certain cases, we've provided suggestions on how the family can also enjoy the meal as a side dish.
- KEEP THINGS SMOOTH. At this stage, babies prefer their food to be very smooth, meaning no chunks or graininess. Save the chunkiness for your baby's legs! When it comes to their food, the smoother, the better.
- FOLLOW THE FOUR-DAY WAIT RULE. Introduce only one food at a time, waiting at least four days for signs of allergy or aversion. If baby shows no signs of upset after this period, you can introduce a new food or ingredient.

- WATCH FOR BABY'S CUES. If baby is becoming upset, turning her head, or batting the spoon away, don't force it. This process of eating is new to them and can be overwhelming at first.
- DON'T GIVE UP ON CERTAIN FOODS RIGHT AWAY. If your baby doesn't take to a certain food on her first try, it might be tempting to believe she doesn't like that particular food. This is not true. Research shows it can take babies up to twenty times of exposure to the same food before they acquire a taste for it! They are not necessarily saying they don't like the food, but that it is unfamiliar.
- TAKE A LAIDBACK APPROACH. Don't worry about the funny faces your baby makes as she eats. She's never tried food before, and all these new tastes are foreign, but it doesn't mean she doesn't like a particular food. The important thing here is that you are open minded and patient. And, as silly as it might sound, smile and keep your voice positive! Babies are very responsive to the faces and emotions of their parents, so if you keep a great attitude, chances are that they will follow suit.
- TEXTURE IS IMPORTANT. Oftentimes, if a baby doesn't seem to favor a particular food, it's more about the consistency or texture of the food rather than the taste. Be ready to add more breast milk, formula, or water to thin the puree, or blend it until it is a finer consistency, then try again.

Note: We start this book at 6 months because that is generally when babies begin eating food other than breast milk or formula, but many times baby will be ready to eat at 5 or even 4 months. Always consult your baby's pediatrician before starting your baby on solid food.

Look for the following icons on each recipe to determine how it can be served:

PUREE   MASHED   SPOON FEED   SELF FEED   FAMILY FRIENDLY

BUTTERNUT SQUASH
IN THE BUFF

AGE 6 months plus
YIELD approximately 3 cups
FOOD STORAGE refrigerator friendly, freezer friendly
PREP TIME 5 minutes
COOK TIME 45 minutes

Butternut squash is an excellent first food for your baby! It's loaded with vitamin A, and you can use water to easily thin the puree and achieve the desired consistency for your baby. One butternut squash reaps many servings, so you have the option of also serving it to the family or storing it in small containers and freezing. This means you'll have plenty of baby food ready when you need it! This was one of Penelope's favorite first foods.

INGREDIENTS

- 1 medium-size butternut squash
- 1 tablespoon extra virgin olive oil

1 Preheat the oven to 400 degrees.

2 Cut the butternut squash in half lengthwise. Scoop the seeds out with a spoon and discard. Place the squash halves on the baking sheet, flesh side up (skin side down). Brush or drizzle the oil onto the squash, and bake for 40–50 minutes or until you can insert a spoon into the meat of the squash with little resistance. Remove from the oven, and allow it to cool slightly.

3 If the family will also be enjoying this meal, set aside the family's portion at this time. To prepare the baby's portion, use a spoon to scoop the flesh of the squash into a blender or food processor. Add small amounts of water at a time, if needed, and puree to a smooth consistency. Serve to baby.

Note: Younger babies tend to favor a smoother consistency. The family can enjoy this dish as soup if desired. Puree the squash in a blender or food processor, and add small amounts of water as needed. Season the family's portion only with salt, pepper, and cinnamon to taste. Serve and enjoy!

SIMPLE SWEET POTATOES

AGE 6 months plus

YIELD approximately 2 ½ cups

FOOD STORAGE refrigerator friendly, freezer friendly

PREP TIME 5 minutes

COOK TIME 40-50 minutes

We love sweet potatoes for our little ones, and we love them for ourselves too! Sweet potatoes are a delight to your little one's palate, and they are loaded with vitamin A! Baking is our preferred cooking method for this recipe, as it retains the most nutrients and brings out the potato's natural sweetness. This recipe purposely yields a large batch so that you can store and freeze the sweet potatoes for later. Your baby's food will be ready and waiting when you need it!

INGREDIENTS

- 2 medium sweet potatoes

1 Preheat the oven to 400 degrees.

2 Wash the sweet potatoes with soap and warm water to remove any dirt. Pat them dry. Using a fork, poke a few holes in the sweet potatoes and place them in the middle rack of the oven. (Tip: you can place a baking sheet on the lower rack under the potatoes to catch any possible drainage from the potatoes.) Bake for 40–50 minutes or until soft and tender with the prick of a fork.

3 Remove from the oven, and, once they're cool enough to handle, slit the potatoes in half with a knife. If the family will also be enjoying this meal, set aside the family's portion at this time. For the baby's portion, scoop the flesh of the sweet potato into a blender or food processor. Add small amounts of water at a time if needed and puree to the desired consistency.

Note: Younger babies tend to favor a smoother consistency. If the family will also be enjoying this meal, you can serve it like a baked potato, adding butter, salt, and/or cinnamon to taste.

BIRTHDAY SUIT BANANAS

AGE 6 months plus
YIELD 1 serving
FOOD STORAGE best served immediately
PREP TIME 1 minute
COOK TIME no cook!

All you need for this recipe is a banana—the birthday suit is optional! Banana is a fan favorite among babies, and this recipe is about as simple as it gets! Once your baby is used to plain banana, try adding a tiny dash of cinnamon, nutmeg, or cardamom to expose her to new flavors. Since too much banana may cause your baby constipation, we recommend starting with a quarter of a banana and seeing how she does. For overall digestive health, you can try rotating among prunes, pears, and bananas.

INGREDIENTS

- ¼ banana, peeled

1 Place the banana in a small plate and throughly mash it with a fork until smooth. That's it! Serve it to baby.

Note: Younger babies tend to favor a smoother consistency.

ONLY OATS

AGE 6 months plus

YIELD approximately 3 cups (may vary)

FOOD STORAGE refrigerator friendly, freezer friendly

PREP TIME 1 minute

COOK TIME 30 minutes

Oatmeal is a comforting and excellent first food for your baby, and steel cut oats are loaded with fiber! This is a dish that the entire family can enjoy, so make a big pot, store it in an airtight container, and refrigerate or freeze it. Breakfast is ready! Once your baby is used to plain steel cut oats, try mixing them with a little pureed prune, pear, or banana for added flavor!

INGREDIENTS

- Steel cut oats, preferably organic
- Water

1 Follow the instructions on the steel cut oats package, and cook until the oats are tender.

2 If serving this as a family meal, set the family's portion aside. Allow the baby's portion to cool slightly, then transfer the baby's portion to a blender. Add the minimum amount of breast milk, formula, or water needed to puree. Blend until the oatmeal is a smooth consistency. Serve!

Note: Younger babies tend to favor a smoother consistency. You may season the family's portion with ingredients such as cinnamon, nutmeg, cardamom, maple syrup, fresh berries, raisins, and/or chopped nuts.

VELVETY PRUNES

AGE 6 months plus
YIELD approximately ½ cup
FOOD STORAGE refrigerator friendly, freezer friendly
PREP TIME 8 minutes
COOK TIME no cook!

Prunes, also known as dried plums, are a fiber powerhouse! They are gentle on baby's stomach and may help ease constipation. Prunes have a smooth, velvety texture when pureed. Try serving prunes plain to your baby first, and as the days go on, you can try mixing them with oatmeal or another fruit or vegetable your baby enjoys. This recipe makes several servings so that you can store it in small containers, freeze, and have baby food ready when you need it!

INGREDIENTS

- 8 pitted prunes (dried plums)
- ¼–½ cup warm water

1 Place prunes in a bowl with warm water (enough to cover the prunes). Soak the prunes for 5 minutes.

2 Drain and place prunes in a blender or food processor with water. (Begin with ¼ cup water and add more as needed.) Puree to a smooth consistency. Serve!

Note: Younger babies tend to favor a smoother consistency. You may add pureed prunes to an adult smoothie, to assist with overall digestive health.

CLEAN CARROTS

AGE 6 months plus
YIELD approximately ¾ cup
FOOD STORAGE refrigerator friendly, freezer friendly
PREP TIME 4 minutes
COOK TIME 7 minutes

Carrots are a favorite of ours, and they're extremely high in vitamin A! We like to steam carrots to preserve the nutrients. This recipe purposely makes several servings for you to store, freeze, and defrost as needed.

INGREDIENTS

- 2 cups water
- 1 cup carrots, peeled and chopped

1 Boil the water in a medium saucepan. Add the carrots, cover, and steam for about 5–7 minutes, reducing heat if needed. The carrots are ready when they are soft and tender with the prick of a fork.

2 Drain the carrots and place in a blender or food processor. Puree until smooth, adding water by ½ cup at a time to achieve the desired consistency. Serve to your baby.

Note: Younger babies tend to favor a smoother consistency.

PLAIN PEAS

AGE 6 months plus

YIELD approximately 2 cups

FOOD STORAGE refrigerator friendly, freezer friendly

PREP TIME 1 minute

COOK TIME 10 minutes

Did you know that peas are an excellent source of vitamin C for your little one? They are also a good source of vitamin A and fiber, making them a wonderful first food for your brand new eater! Like all first foods, try serving the peas plain first. After several days, you can mix them into some of your baby's favorite foods to change things up! We like using frozen organic peas for ease and convenience. This recipe purposely yields several servings so that the family can also enjoy a side vegetable, or store the puree in small containers, freeze, and defrost for baby as needed.

INGREDIENTS

- ½ cup water
- 1 (16-ounce) package frozen peas, preferably organic

1 Bring the water to a boil in a medium saucepan. Add the peas, stir gently, and return to a boil. Cover the pan, reduce the heat, and simmer for 5–7 minutes or until the peas are tender.

2 Drain and place the peas in a blender or food processor. Puree, adding small amounts of water as needed to achieve the desired consistency.

Note: Younger babies tend to favor a smoother consistency. If the family will also be enjoying this meal, set aside the family's portion prior to pureeing, and season with salt and pepper if desired.

BARE PEAR

AGE 6 months plus

YIELD approximately ½ cup

FOOD STORAGE best served immediately, refrigerator friendly for up to 24 hrs

PREP TIME 2 minutes

COOK TIME no cook!

Pears are delicious and mild on little tummies, and they're an excellent source of fiber! You can try them plain, or stir them into your baby's oatmeal for added texture and flavor. Pears tend to turn brown quickly, so you can optionally squeeze a little bit of lemon juice on top to minimize the browning.

INGREDIENTS

- ¼ ripe pear, preferably organic, core and seeds removed

1 Place the pear in blender or food processor and puree, adding small amounts of water as needed to achieve the desired consistency.

Note: Younger babies tend to favor a smoother consistency. Pear tends to brown quickly, so to store any leftovers, sprinkle fresh lemon juice over the pear, store in an airtight container, and refrigerate.

CREAMY AVOCADO

AGE 6 months plus

YIELD approximately ½ cup

FOOD STORAGE best served immediately, refrigerator friendly for up to 24 hrs

PREP TIME 3 minutes

COOK TIME no cook!

Avocados are an excellent source of healthy fats and vitamins for your baby, making them a wonderful first food! For some babies, the texture is an acquired one. If your baby doesn't wolf down avocado the first couple of times you try it, don't get discouraged. Research shows it can take up to 20 tries for a baby to warm up and familiarize himself with a particular food! You can try mixing the mashed avocado with a little breast milk, formula, or one of your baby's favorite purees to create a consistency he might enjoy. To store the other half of the avocado, sprinkle fresh lemon juice over the flesh and store it in an airtight container in the fridge. Alternatively, try the delicious Cocoa Avocado Smoothie for Parent (recipe to follow) to make great use of the other half and feed yourself!

INGREDIENTS

- ½ avocado, skin and seed removed
- ½ teaspoon fresh lemon juice, seeds removed

1 In a small plate, thoroughly mash the avocado with a fork to a consistency your baby will enjoy. Add the lemon juice to the avocado and mix well to incorporate. Serve to your baby.

Note: Younger babies tend to favor a smoother consistency.

COCOA AVOCADO
SMOOTHIE FOR PARENT

AGE for adults!

YIELD 1 serving for parent

FOOD STORAGE best served immediately, refrigerator friendly for up to 24 hours

PREP TIME 5 minutes

COOK TIME no cook!

This recipe is for you! Ali's daughter, Penelope, usually only ate half of an avocado, so she created this shake for herself using the other half. The result was this delicious, healthy, creamy smoothie that she could take to go, and it would satisfy her appetite until dinner! A recipe that takes care of lunch for both of you? That's a win-win in our book!

INGREDIENTS

- ½ avocado
- 1 ripe banana, peeled
- 1 cup almond milk (or your preferred milk of choice)
- ½ teaspoon ground cinnamon
- 1 tablespoon local honey
- 2 teaspoons raw cocoa powder
- 3 ice cubes (For an extra kick, try using "coffee cubes" by freezing brewed coffee in an ice cube tray. This is a great pick-me-up for busy, tired parents!)

1 Using a spoon, scoop the flesh out from the avocado and place in a blender. Add all the remaining ingredients, and blend until smooth. Serve to yourself, and enjoy!

SAMPLE FOOD SCHEDULE
FOR 8-MONTH-OLD BABY

The following feeding schedule is a sample of what one mom feeds her 8-month-old baby. This is simply one example that is intended to act as a guide only. All babies have different feeding times and eat different quantities. We recommend that you consult your pediatrician with any questions or concerns with regards to feeding your baby.

If a food name is italicized, that means you'll find the recipe in this book.

7:00 A.M. (BREAKFAST):	8 ounces breast milk or formula
11:00 A.M. (LUNCH):	4–5 tablespoons solid foods, such as *Blueberries with Spinach* or *Baby Green Machine* 6–7 ounces breast milk or formula
3:00 P.M. (SNACK):	4–5 tablespoons solid foods, such as *Bananas with Cinnamon* or *Fruity Fusion* 6–7 ounces breast milk or formula
6:00 P.M. (DINNER):	4–5 tablespoons solid foods, such as *Roasted Salmon with Pear and Lime* or *Iron Chicken Dance* 8 ounces breast milk or formula

Tip: Try feeding your baby a "rainbow" of solid foods throughout the day so that she gets a variety of nutrition. For example, if you serve something green for lunch, try serving something yellow for a snack, something orange for dinner, etc.

8 MONTHS PLUS:
STACKING UP

We referred to our last section of single-ingredient recipes as the "building blocks," and now the fun begins: it's time to start stacking! Here is where plain old peas are served up with an Italian twist, standard oatmeal is complemented with yummy vanilla and cardamom, and simple fruits are spun into savory, smoothie-like purees that will be a pure delight for your little one—and you!

We also introduce fish and meats in this section in puree form, so that little eaters will have an easy time working these new tastes and textures around their tiny mouths.

The main points to remember during this stage are:

- YOUR BABY'S INDEPENDENCE IS GROWING. Your baby may begin trying to feed himself at this stage by grabbing the spoon and/or attempting to pick up pieces of food with his fingers. Encourage him to explore!
- BE AWARE OF TEXTURES. Lots of times, if a baby rejects something, it is due to texture, not taste. Place baby's portion back into the blender or food processor, add more water if needed, and try again.
- KEEP THESE RECIPES IN MIND FOR LATER. Lots of these recipes can be served in a nonpureed form as your baby gets more comfortable with textures and self-feeding, so keep her favorites in mind as she grows.
- FREEZE FOOD FOR LATER—EVEN IF SHE DIDN'T LIKE IT! Utilize your freezer even if you feel your baby didn't enjoy something! It is common that she will later gobble up a food she seemed uninterested in previously.

Look for the following icons on each recipe to determine how it can be served:

PUREE   MASHED   SPOON FEED   SELF FEED   FAMILY FRIENDLY

ROASTED SALMON WITH
PEAR AND LIME

AGE 8 months plus
YIELD approximately 2 cups
FOOD STORAGE refrigerator friendly, freezer friendly
PREP TIME 3 minutes
COOK TIME 7 minutes

A gastronomic and healthy delight, this meal is amazingly easy to prepare and is extremely nutritious. In this single dish, your baby gains the health benefits of omegas, DHA, fiber, and citrus. If at first your baby seems reluctant to eat this, try mixing it with a fruit or vegetable puree that you know your baby enjoys, such as pureed apple, sweet potato, or additional pureed pear. Store any remaining puree in small containers, freeze, and defrost as needed.

"This is a very good source of omega-3 fatty acids, which are important to your baby's neuro and cognitive develop-ment."—JuliSu DiMucci-Ward, registered dietitian and pediatric specialist in nutrition.

INGREDIENTS

- 2 Wild Alaskan Salmon fillets, skin on, each about 6 ounces
- 1 ripe pear, skin on, core and seeds removed, roughly chopped
- Juice of 1 lime, seeds removed

1 Preheat the oven to 400 degrees.

2 Line a baking sheet with foil, and place the salmon on the baking sheet, skin side down (flesh side up). Roast the salmon in the oven for 7–10 minutes or until it is fully cooked and flakes apart easily with a fork.

3 Remove the skin from the salmon and transfer the fish to a blender. Add the pear and lime juice to the blender. Puree, adding small amounts of water at a time if needed to create a consistency your baby will enjoy. Serve!

Note: Younger babies tend to favor a smoother consistency.

Lime is an excellent source of vitamin C.

FRUITY FUSION

AGE 8 months plus
YIELD approximately 1 cup
FOOD STORAGE refrigerator friendly, freezer friendly
PREP TIME 5 minutes
COOK TIME no cook!

This puree tastes so delicious, even adults will want to eat a few spoonfuls! The sweetness of the apple and pear balanced with the tartness of lime creates a very satisfying taste experience. This is a wonderful and nutrition-packed option for lunch or a snack.

INGREDIENTS

- ½ apple, roughly chopped with skin on, core and seeds removed
- ½ a ripe pear, roughly chopped with skin on, core and seeds removed
- ½ an avocado, skin and seed removed
- ½ cup tightly packed fresh baby spinach leaves, preferably organic
- 1½ teaspoons fresh lime juice, seeds removed

1 Add all the ingredients to a blender and puree, adding small amounts of water at a time if needed. Puree to a consistency your baby will enjoy, and serve!

Note: Younger babies tend to favor a smoother consistency.

Lime is an excellent source of vitamin C.

BLUEBERRIES WITH
SPINACH

AGE 8 months plus
YIELD approximately ½ cup
FOOD STORAGE refrigerator friendly
PREP TIME 3 minutes
COOK TIME no cook!

This was one of Landon's very first foods, and he devoured it! Blueberries and spinach are nutrition-packed foods, and together their flavor is quite delicious! Expect this puree to be a dark brown/purple color due to the blueberries.

"This is an especially effective recipe because vitamin C in the blueberries aids the absorption of iron from the spinach, allowing your baby to benefit from even more nutrients out of every bite!"—Dr. Elissa Levine, pediatrician.

INGREDIENTS

- ½ cup blueberries, preferably organic
- 1 cup tightly packed fresh baby spinach, preferably organic

1 Add the ingredients to the blender and puree thoroughly until smooth, adding small amounts of water if needed to achieve a consistency your baby will enjoy. Serve!

Note: Younger babies tend to favor a smoother consistency.

BANANAS WITH CINNAMON

AGE 8 months plus
YIELD approximately ¼ cup
FOOD STORAGE best served immediately
PREP TIME 3 minutes
COOK TIME no cook!

This recipe is our Birthday Suit Bananas recipe with the volume turned up, and it's one of the simplest examples of how to introduce a new flavor to broaden your baby's palate. We encourage you to play with flavors and substitute the cinnamon with ground nutmeg or ground cardamom from time to time.

INGREDIENTS

- ½ banana, peeled
- ⅛ teaspoon ground cinnamon

1 In a small plate, mash the banana to a consistency your baby will enjoy. Add the ground cinnamon and mix thoroughly. Serve immediately.

Note: Younger babies tend to favor a smoother consistency.

Cinnamon can help reduce inflammation, has antioxidant and antiseptic properties, and can help fight bacteria

PLEASE MORE PEAS

AGE 8 months plus
YIELD approximately 3 cups
FOOD STORAGE refrigerator friendly, freezer friendly
PREP TIME 5 minutes
COOK TIME 15 minutes

This recipe presents peas with a delightful Italian twist, and it's a wonderful building block on our Plain Peas recipe. With flavor hints of garlic and lemon, this recipe is a delicious vegetable side dish the entire family can enjoy!

INGREDIENTS

Garlic is used to build the immune system.

- 2 tablespoons extra virgin olive oil
- ½ yellow onion, diced
- 1 teaspoon fresh garlic, minced (about 1 clove)
- 1 pound frozen green peas, straight from the freezer
- 1 cup low sodium vegetable broth, preferably organic
- 1 teaspoon kosher salt (optional: we recommend adding salt only if your child is 12 mo+)
- ¼ teaspoon black pepper
- 1½ tablespoons fresh lemon juice, seeds removed

1 Heat the oil in a medium saucepan over medium heat. When the oil is hot, add the onions and sauté for 4–6 minutes or until the onions are soft and translucent. Add the garlic and stir continuously for 30 seconds to prevent burning.

2 Add the peas, vegetable broth, salt (if using), and pepper. Stir the ingredients to combine well and bring to a boil. Once boiling, reduce the heat to medium low, stir occasionally, and cook the peas for 2–3 additional minutes or until the peas are tender and soft. Add the lemon juice and mix well.

3 Puree, using the cooking liquid and a small amount of water if needed, or place a few peas on your baby's high chair tray if you feel he is capable of self-feeding.

Note: If the family will also be enjoying this meal, set aside the family's portion prior to pureeing, and season with additional salt and pepper if desired.

SOW YOUR OATS?

AGE 8 months plus
YIELD approximately 3 ½ cups
FOOD STORAGE refrigerator friendly, freezer friendly
PREP TIME 2 minutes
COOK TIME 30 minutes

This recipe is inspired by Amy's mother, who makes a large pot of these spiced oats for the family when all of her kids come to visit. Subtle flavors of vanilla, cardamom, and nutmeg awaken plain ol' oats and fill the house with enticing aromas that lure the family to the table. Amy often makes a large batch of these oats on Sunday, stores it in the refrigerator, and the whole family has a nutritious breakfast ready and waiting for several days! Once your baby reaches 12 months plus (or once he is fully transitioned to dairy milk), you can try making this recipe with half milk and half water for a delicious, creamy texture that is pleasing and comforting!

INGREDIENTS

- 5 cups of water
- 1 cup steel cut oats, preferably organic
- 1 teaspoon vanilla extract
- ¼ teaspoon ground cardamom
- ¼ teaspoon ground nutmeg

1 Bring the water to a boil in a medium saucepan. Add the oats, vanilla, cardamom, and nutmeg. Stir to blend well. Reduce the heat to medium low and simmer the oats, stirring occasionally, for 25–30 minutes or until the oats are tender.

2 Serve slightly warm or at room temperature. The oats will thicken over time, so to serve leftovers, add a little water or breast milk, mix, reheat, and serve.

Cardamom may help ease stomach & intestinal gas

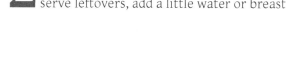

BUTTERNUT SQUASH WITH
ROSEMARY AND SAGE

AGE 8 months plus
YIELD approximately 4 cups
FOOD STORAGE refrigerator friendly, freezer friendly
PREP TIME approximately 5 minutes with precut butternut squash
COOK TIME approximately 30 minutes

One day, Amy came home to find her husband feeding their 8-month-old son Landon an intriguing, bright-orange-colored puree with little green specs. Landon was walloping down the contents of his spoon. "What are you feeding him?!" Amy inquired. "I cooked him butternut squash with rosemary and sage," her husband replied. Amy was impressed! It was this recipe that helped inspire the collaboration for this cookbook.

INGREDIENTS

- 5 cups butternut squash, chopped into ½-inch-by-½-inch cubes (for time savings, check if your market sells this precut)
- 2 teaspoons extra virgin olive oil
- 1 teaspoon fresh sage leaves, finely minced
- ½ teaspoon fresh rosemary, finely minced
- ¼ teaspoon kosher salt (optional: we recommend adding salt only if your baby is 12 months plus.)

1 Preheat the oven to 350 degrees.

2 In a large mixing bowl, add the squash, oil, sage, rosemary, and salt (if using). Toss to mix well. Place the butternut squash on a baking sheet lined with foil, and spread the cubes into a single layer. Roast the squash for 30–35 minutes or until the cubes are soft and tender with the prick of a fork.

3 Puree the squash, adding small amounts of water at a time if needed, or serve bite-size pieces to your child, cutting the cubes into smaller pieces if necessary.

Rosemary may help boost the immune system & improve blood circulation

BABY GREEN MACHINE

AGE 8 months plus
YIELD approximately 3-4 cups
FOOD STORAGE refrigerator friendly for up to 5–7 days, freezer friendly
PREP TIME 10 minutes
COOK TIME 10 minutes

Many parents would love their baby to reap the nutritional benefits of kale, but many are unsure how to prepare it and entice their little one to eat it! This recipe blends powerhouse kale with the natural sweetness of apple and a hint of lemon. As your baby transitions into toddlerhood and becomes too old for purees, try adding more water to make this recipe a delicious juice! This yields quite a few servings so that you can store them in small containers, freeze, and defrost as needed, or consider setting aside a portion and creating a juice for you!

"I love this recipe for combining an iron-rich green (kale) with the vitamin C of the lemon juice to make the iron more bioavailable. While eating excessive amounts of dark, leafy greens can contribute to thyroid problems, normal portion sizes several times per week should not be an issue for healthy infants and children."—Dr. Elissa Levine, pediatrician.

INGREDIENTS

- Approximately 1 cup of water, divided
- 1 medium-size bunch of organic kale, rinsed with stems removed (approximately 4 cups)
- 2 medium-size apples, seeds and cores removed, cut into chunks (about 2 cups)
- Juice from 1 fresh-squeezed lemon, seeds removed (about ⅓ cup)

Tip: To easily stem kale, plug a clean sink and fill about one-third full with water, or fill a large bowl one-third full with water. Place kale leaves in the water and "swoosh" them around to loosen and remove any dirt. Then, with one hand holding the leaf upside down by the tip of the rib, use your other hand to pull the leaf away from the rib. Discard the ribs.

Even better tip: Check your local supermarket for packaged kale that has already been stemmed to save yourself even more time!

1 Place a medium saucepan on the stove and fill with about ½ cup of water. Bring water to a boil, then add the kale leaves. Allow the kale to soften and deflate for about 2 minutes. Gently stir with tongs, then place the lid on the pot and allow the kale to steam and soften for 3–5 minutes.

2 Allow the kale to cool slightly, then transfer to a blender or food processor. Add apple, lemon juice, approximately ½ cup of water or more if needed, and puree to achieve the desired consistency. Serve!

Lemon is an excellent source of vitamin C.

GENTLE GINGER MEDLEY

AGE 8 months plus
YIELD approximately 6-8 cups
FOOD STORAGE refrigerator friendly, freezer friendly
PREP TIME 10 minutes
COOK TIME 25 minutes

This sweet, creamy, superfood puree is a nutritious dish your baby is sure to love! You can puree the entire recipe for baby, or set half aside before pureeing for the family to enjoy. Ali felt more at ease serving Penelope broccoli, which has gotten a bad rap for being "gassy," because this dish mixes in ginger, which has stomach-settling properties to balance things out.

INGREDIENTS

- Approximately 2½ cups water, divided
- 2 medium-size sweet potatoes, peeled and cut into ½-inch chunks
- 1 (16 ounce) package frozen broccoli florets
- 2 medium-size apples, seeds and stems removed, cut into chunks (removing skin is optional; we prefer to leave it on if organic)
- 1-inch-by-½-inch piece of fresh ginger, peeled and minced

1 Bring 2 cups of water to a boil in a large saucepan. Add the sweet potatoes, return to a boil, and cover with a lid until the potatoes are soft and tender (about 5–7 minutes).

2 Add the frozen broccoli, another ½ cup of water, and stir. Cover and boil until the broccoli is soft and cooked (about 8–10 minutes). Remove from the heat.

3 Allow the vegetables to slightly cool, then add the apple and ginger, and gently stir to combine. (If the family or a toddler will also be enjoying this meal, set aside their portions at this time.) Place the baby's portion in a blender or food processor and puree, adding water by the ¼ cup if necessary to achieve the desired consistency for your baby. Serve!

Ginger is an antioxidant & helps support the immune system

CINNAMON SPICE AND
EVERYTHING RICE

AGE 8 months plus

YIELD approximately 2½ cups

FOOD STORAGE refrigerator friendly, freezer friendly

PREP TIME 5 minutes

COOK TIME 40 minutes

The first time Ali fed this to Penelope, she was 8-months-old, and she went absolutely crazy for it! She couldn't feed it to her fast enough. When you taste it, you'll see why! Even now as a toddler, it is still one of her favorite meals! We love cooking this dish because it makes our kitchens smell delicious, and we can't help ourselves from eating a spoonful every time! This recipe yields quite a few servings, so it's perfect for storing and having it ready when you need it.

INGREDIENTS

- ½ cup whole grain jasmine rice*
- 2 cups water
- 1 cup carrots (scrub skin thoroughly to remove any dirt), chopped
- 1 medium-size organic apple (about 1½ cups), chopped, skin on, stem and seeds removed
- 1 cup coconut milk
- 1 teaspoon ground cinnamon

1 Prepare ½ cup of rice as instructed by the package.

2 In the meantime, bring 2 cups of water to a boil in a large frying pan. Add the carrots, cover, and steam for 5–7 minutes or until soft and tender. Allow to cool slightly.

3 Place cooked rice, apples, steamed carrots, coconut milk, and cinnamon in a blender. Puree to desired consistency. If serving as a side dish for the family, mix the ingredients together and set the family's portion aside before pureeing.

For taste purposes, we prefer jasmine rice for this recipe, but feel free to use any rice you desire. Follow the cooking directions on your rice package to prepare. Keep in mind that cook time will vary based on the rice used.

Cinnamon can help reduce inflammation, has antioxidant and antiseptic properties, and can help fight bacteria

THE IRON CHICKEN DANCE

AGE 8 months plus
YIELD approximately 4-6 chicken thighs
FOOD STORAGE refrigerator friendly, freezer friendly
PREP TIME 8 minules
COOK TIME 40 minutes

We call this one the Iron Chicken Dance because the chicken thighs are nutrient rich, packing all the iron we know is so important for our babies' little bodies, and the salsa makes it "dance." Don't be intimidated by the term "salsa"—it's super easy to toss together! This recipe makes for an excellent family meal!

INGREDIENTS

- 1½ pounds boneless, skinless chicken thighs, preferably organic
- ½ teaspoon kosher salt (optional: we only recommend adding salt for babies 12 months plus)
- ½ teaspoon pepper
- ½ teaspoon dried herb mixture, such as Herbes de Provence or Italian seasoning
- 2 tablespoons extra virgin olive oil
- ½ tablespoon unsalted butter
- 1 (15-ounce) can organic black beans, rinsed and drained
- 2 cups fresh mango, diced into ½-inch-by-½-inch chunks (for time savings, check if your market sells this precut)
- ¼ cup fresh cilantro, minced
- Juice from 1 lime, seeds removed

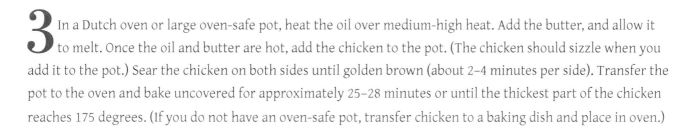

Cilantro can help rid the body of harmful toxins

1 Preheat the oven to 350 degrees.

2 Season both sides of the chicken with salt (if using), pepper, and dried herbs. Set aside.

3 In a Dutch oven or large oven-safe pot, heat the oil over medium-high heat. Add the butter, and allow it to melt. Once the oil and butter are hot, add the chicken to the pot. (The chicken should sizzle when you add it to the pot.) Sear the chicken on both sides until golden brown (about 2–4 minutes per side). Transfer the pot to the oven and bake uncovered for approximately 25–28 minutes or until the thickest part of the chicken reaches 175 degrees. (If you do not have an oven-safe pot, transfer chicken to a baking dish and place in oven.)

4 Remove the pot from the oven and add the black beans. Cover the pot with a lid and let the mixture rest for 5 minutes. Add the mango, cilantro, and lime juice to the pot. Serve, cutting into smaller pieces appropriate for your baby, or puree the baby's portion to desired consistency, adding small amounts of water as needed.

Tip: If your baby seems hesitant or generally has a difficult time eating meats, try mixing in 1 teaspoon of sour cream. If she still seems hesitant, puree a small portion of the dish and spread it on a slice of whole wheat bread, creating a "pâté sandwich." This may help make meats more palatable to babies/toddlers adjusting to the new texture.

CAULIFLOWER APPLE STEAMER

AGE 8 months plus
YIELD approximately 4 cups
FOOD STORAGE refrigerator friendly
PREP TIME 10 minutes
COOK TIME 7 minutes

Babies of all ages seem to love this one, thanks to the versatility between pureeing and serving as a finger food. Penelope still enjoys it as a toddler. Cauliflower is packed with a surprising amount of vitamin C and fiber, and the apple offers complementary nutrients and sweetness.

INGREDIENTS

- 1 head organic cauliflower, chopped into small florets (approximately 1–1½ pounds; you may also use 1 (16-ounce) bag of frozen cauliflower)
- 1 medium-size apple, core and stem removed, diced into ½-inch-by-½-inch cubes
- 1 tablespoon extra virgin olive oil
- ¼ teaspoon salt (optional: we only recommend adding salt for babies 12 months plus)
- ¼ teaspoon pepper

1 In a large skillet, bring approximately ¼ inch of water to a boil. Add the cauliflower, cover, and steam until the florets are soft and tender (about 3–5 minutes). Add the apple, remove from the heat, cover, and allow the cauliflower to sit for an additional 2 minutes. Allow the mixture to cool slightly.

2 In a large mixing bowl, add the oil, salt, and pepper, and stir to combine. Add the cauliflower and apple to the bowl, and toss well to coat. If pureeing, add all the contents to a blender and puree, adding water by the ¼ cup to achieve the desired consistency. If serving as a finger food, chop into bite-size pieces appropriate for your baby. Serve!

Pepper may help fight germs & increase the flow of digestive juices in the stomach.

BEET RED LENTILS

AGE 8 months plus
YIELD approximately 4 cups
FOOD STORAGE refrigerator friendly, freezer friendly
PREP TIME 10 minutes
COOK TIME 25 minutes

Beets, the star of this dish, are a powerhouse food for many reasons: they are known to ease digestion, help with constipation, and even help provide relief from congestion! The other rock stars of this puree are the lentils, which provide a nice source of protein for your baby. Coriander, ginger, apple, and mint add many complementary benefits, reducing inflammation, calming the stomach, and relieving gas. Phew! This one is truly a nourishing recipe! Don't be alarmed at your baby's reddish urine or stools in the next day or two after feeding her this dish; that's just the beet pigment coming through your baby's system, and it's perfectly safe. Use a full-coverage bib when feeding baby, as beets can stain.

"I love introducing babies to lentils and beans, although it can be a difficult texture for your baby to accept at first. When babies refuse foods, remember that it is often because they don't like the texture, not the taste. Blending lentils with beets introduces this new texture in a more 'baby-friendly' way. Don't take an initial refusal as a sign that your baby does not like lentils. Some babies need to be exposed to a new food up to a dozen times before they will accept it. So keep trying!"—Dr. Elissa Levine, pediatrician.

INGREDIENTS

- 3 beets, washed, peeled, and quartered, greens and stems removed*
- 1 cup red lentils, rinsed and picked over (remove any unwanted debris)
- 1 medium organic apple, core and seeds removed, quartered
- ¾ inch fresh ginger, roughly chopped
- 1 tablespoon chopped fresh mint
- ½ teaspoon ground coriander

You can save the beet greens and juice them for yourself, or add to a stir-fry!

1 Place the beets in a small pot with just enough water to cover them entirely. Cover with a lid, and boil on high heat for 18–20 minutes or until you can insert a fork into the beets with no resistance. Strain the beets, reserving the cooking water. Set aside.

2 Place the lentils in a medium-size pot, and boil with water according to package instructions. Strain the lentils.

3 Add the cooked beets, cooked lentils, and all remaining ingredients in a blender or food processor. Add ½ cup of the reserved beets' cooking water, and blend to desired consistency. Add additional cooking water or regular water by the ½ cup as needed. Serve!

The oil in mint is thought to calm the stomach and reduce gas.

SAMPLE FOOD SCHEDULE
FOR 10-MONTH-OLD BABY

The following feeding schedule is a sample of what one mom feeds her 10-month-old baby. This is simply one example that is intended to act as a guide only. All babies have different feeding times and eat different quantities. We recommend that you consult your pediatrician with any questions or concerns with regards to feeding your baby.

If a food name is italicized, that means you'll find the recipe in this book.

7:00 A.M. (BREAKFAST):	8 ounces breast milk or formula
10:00 A.M. (SNACK):	2–3 tablespoons solid food, such as *Strawberry Banana Greek Yogurt* 5–6 ounces breast milk or formula
1:00 P.M. (LUNCH):	2–3 tablespoons solid food, such as *Kheema: Indian Ground Beef* or *Warm Lentils with Cumin and Coriander* 5–6 ounces breast milk or formula
4:00 P.M. (SNACK):	2–3 tablespoons solid food, such as *Kale with Garlic and Ginger* 5–6 ounces breast milk or formula
6:00 P.M. (DINNER):	2–3 tablespoons solid food, such as *Coconut Curry Goan Fish* or *Dance Party Chicken Nuggets* 5–6 ounces breast milk or formula

Tip: Try feeding your baby a "rainbow" of solid foods throughout the day so that she gets a variety of nutrition. For example, if you serve something green for lunch, try serving something yellow for a snack, something orange for dinner, etc. To maintain a balanced diet, try feeding your baby a fruit, a vegetable, a protein, and a grain through the course of the day.

10 MONTHS PLUS:
FLAVORS, FAMILY, & INDEPENDENCE

This stage is exciting for many reasons: chunkier textures, your baby's adorable attempts to feed herself, and even more yummy flavors, just to name a few!

This is where you, the parent, can get creative, as you are now hopefully gaining confidence in feeding your little one. Don't be afraid to blend flavors together—even if it may not sound appealing to you! While we were feeding our own babies, one pediatrician recommended that things that may sound unappetizing to us (like peas mixed with blueberries, or some other weird combination) may be absolutely delicious to a baby! We shouldn't let our preconceived notions of food get in the way of different combinations we try for them.

We also begin to get the most taste and health benefits from our favorite herbs and spices: cinnamon, nutmeg, garlic, ginger, parsley, rosemary, turmeric, coriander, and more. Your kitchen is going to smell amazing! You'll be happy to find meals here that will work for the whole family, such as *Warm Lentils with Cumin and Coriander*, *Mediterranean Couscous with Feta, Lemon and Parsley*, and *Coconut Curry Goan Fish.*

The main points to remember during this stage are:

- LET YOUR BABY EXPLORE. To us, it is of course a giant mess. But your baby is truly learning when he gets in and gets dirty, so as hard as it may be to watch, let him have at it. Take a deep breath as he "becomes one" with his food, get the bath ready, and remember that this stage shall pass!

- TRY, TRY AGAIN. You might believe that your baby doesn't like a certain food that he tried in the earlier stages, which could make you leery of a recipe that includes that particular ingredient. Don't be! It takes numerous attempts for a baby to truly like or dislike something. Timing and preparation can make all the difference.

- DON'T EXPECT PREDICTABILITY. Babies' appetites may wax and wane, they may reject an old favorite, or you might worry about their nutrition. There is a lot going on in this stage, so try not to worry so much about any one thing. Visit our "Helpful Tips" chapter for concerns and trouble-shooting tips. And if something is truly bothering you, it's always best to ask your child's pediatrician.

- KEEP A BLENDER HANDY. You might find that your baby isn't ready for the texture of the food you are eating but will still enjoy the taste. We recommend keeping a blender handy so that if your baby seems reluctant to try what you are eating, you can toss it in the blender and create a puree, adding liquid to create the consistency your baby will enjoy. This can work for both bite-size foods as well as purees. For example, if you are serving bite-size foods and it seems your baby is having a hard time with the texture, you can place them in the blender with liquid and make them into a puree. We've had great success using this tactic with our babies!

Look for the following icons on each recipe to determine how it can be served:

PUREE	MASHED	SPOON FEED	SELF FEED	FAMILY FRIENDLY

ROASTED CAULIFLOWER
WITH LEMON & CILANTRO

AGE 10 months plus

YIELD approximately 2 ½ cups

FOOD STORAGE refrigerator friendly, freezer friendly

PREP TIME 10 minutes

COOK TIME 35 minutes

The first time Amy watched her son Landon pop these cauliflower pieces into his mouth like there was no tomorrow, her jaw just about hit the ground! Roasting cauliflower slightly sweetens it, and the acidity of the lemon complements it wonderfully. This is a great food for little hands to start practicing self-feeding with! If your child seems hesitant to eat this at first, you can try adding a little grated cheese on top.

INGREDIENTS

- 4–5 cups fresh cauliflower (about 1 head of cauliflower), chopped into small florets
- 1½ tablespoons extra virgin olive oil
- ¼ teaspoon kosher salt (optional: we recommend adding salt only if your child is 12 months plus)
- ¼ teaspoon black pepper
- 2 teaspoons fresh lemon juice, seeds removed
- 1 tablespoon fresh cilantro, minced

1 Preheat the oven to 350 degrees.

2 In a large mixing bowl, add the cauliflower florets, oil, salt (if using), and pepper. Toss to mix well. Spread the cauliflower on a baking sheet lined with foil, and arrange it in a single layer. Roast in the oven for 30–35 minutes or until soft and tender, tossing the cauliflower once after about 15 minutes.

3 Remove from the oven and add the lemon juice and cilantro. Toss to mix well. Serve bite-size pieces to your child, cutting into smaller pieces if needed.

Cilantro can help rid the body of harmful toxins

ACORN SQUASH WITH
CINNAMON AND NUTMEG

AGE 10 months plus
YIELD 1 acorn squash
FOOD STORAGE refrigerator friendly
PREP TIME 7 minutes
COOK TIME 60 minutes

This recipe is a seasonal treat that many young children look forward to during fall and Thanksgiving. Acorn squash is naturally sweet, and this recipe presents the vegetable with warm flavors of cinnamon and nutmeg, almost reminiscent of a pumpkin pie! You can feel guiltless about eating this delectable vegetable, as acorn squash is an excellent source of vitamin C and potassium. Make this an enjoyable experience for older toddlers by allowing them to eat the squash right out of the shell! To store any leftovers, simply place the shell in an airtight container and store in the refrigerator.

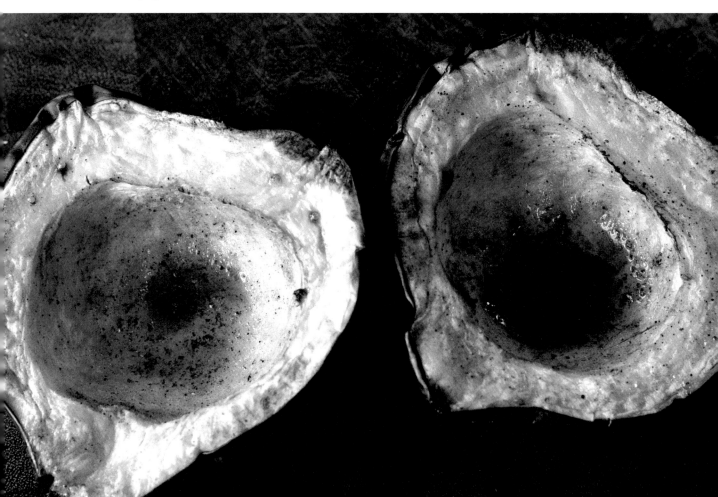

INGREDIENTS

- 1 acorn squash
- 1½ tablespoons unsalted butter
- ⅛ teaspoon ground cinnamon
- ⅛ teaspoon ground nutmeg

1 Preheat oven to 400 degrees.

2 Cut the squash in half lengthwise. Remove the seeds with a spoon and discard. Place the squash flesh side up (skin side down) on a baking sheet lined with foil.

3 In a small bowl, add the butter and microwave for 20–30 seconds or until the butter is fully melted. Add the cinnamon and nutmeg, then mix well. Using a pastry brush or spoon, "paint" or pour the butter mixture over the squash, coating all the flesh evenly. Roast the squash for 1 hour or until tender with the prick of a fork.

SERVING OPTIONS

- To spoon-feed your baby, use a spoon to remove the flesh of the squash, and transfer the desired portion to a small bowl.

- To allow an older toddler to self-feed, cut the desired portion (both shell and flesh), place it in a bowl or plate, and let him enjoy his dining experience right out of the shell!

Nutmeg is used for diarrhea, nausea, stomach pain, & gas

KALE WITH GARLIC & GINGER

AGE 10 months plus
YIELD approximately 4 cups
FOOD STORAGE refrigerator friendly, freezer friendly
PREP TIME 4 minutes
COOK TIME 25 minutes

This nourishing, immunity-boosting recipe combines superfood kale with the amazing health benefits of ginger and garlic. Amy has fed this dish to her sons on countless occasions, especially when she suspects they are coming down with an illness. Kale is an excellent source of vitamin C, and garlic is often used to build the immune system. This recipe intentionally makes a large batch so that the family can enjoy it as a side vegetable, or you can freeze the kale puree in portions and re-serve to your baby as desired.

If at first your baby seems hesitant, check the consistency of the puree and adjust as needed by pureeing longer and/or adding water. You can also try combining it with one of your baby's favorite purees, such as apple or sweet potato, to get her started.

INGREDIENTS

- 2 tablespoons extra virgin olive oil
- 1 medium yellow onion, diced
- 1 tablespoon fresh garlic, minced
- 1 teaspoon fresh ginger, minced
- 1 pound fresh kale, ribs removed
- 3 cups low-sodium vegetable broth, preferably organic
- 2 teaspoons organic raw apple cider vinegar with the "mother" (see note)
- 1 teaspoon black pepper
- Juice of half a lemon, seeds removed

1 Heat the oil in a large stockpot over medium heat. Add the onion and sauté for 4–6 minutes or until soft and translucent. Add the garlic and ginger, stirring frequently for 1 minute to prevent burning. Add the kale, vegetable stock, apple cider vinegar, and black pepper. Stir and bring the liquid to a boil. Reduce the heat to medium low, cover with a lid, and simmer for 15–20 minutes, stirring occasionally.

2 Add the lemon juice. If the family will also be enjoying this dish, set aside the family's portion at this time. To puree the baby's portion, allow the kale to slightly cool, then transfer the kale, some of the onions, and some of the liquid to a blender or food processor. Puree, adding small amounts of water at a time as needed to create a consistency your baby will enjoy. Serve!

Note: "The 'mother', or good bacteria, in the vinegar is what changes apple cider into vinegar," explains Dr. Elissa Levine, pediatrician. "It is safe to eat but considered 'unsightly' by some. Most commercial vinegars filter out the 'mother' as most general consumers prefer a clear liquid." It's "the mother" in the apple cider vinegar that is full of probiotics and other beneficial bacteria.

Ginger is an antioxidant & helps support the immune system

ZUCCHINI AND SQUASH
BITES WITH ROSEMARY

AGE 10 months plus
YIELD approximately 4 cups
FOOD STORAGE refrigerator friendly, freezer friendly
PREP TIME 10 minutes
COOK TIME 18 minutes

Amy couldn't believe her eyes when she saw her son eating these vegetables eagerly by the palmful! The soft texture of the zucchini and squash complemented by flavors of rosemary and lemon makes this a vegetable that kids of many different ages can enjoy. This recipe yields a large batch so the family can enjoy this as a side vegetable, or you can store the remainder in airtight containers, and your baby's food is ready when you need it!

INGREDIENTS

- 2 cups zucchini, diced into ½-inch-by-½-inch cubes
- 2 cups yellow squash, diced into ½-inch-by-½-inch cubes
- 1 tablespoon extra virgin olive oil
- 1 teaspoon fresh rosemary, finely minced
- 2 teaspoons fresh lemon juice, seeds removed

1 Preheat the oven to 350 degrees.

2 In a medium-size mixing bowl, add the zucchini, squash, oil, rosemary, and lemon juice. Toss to mix well.

3 On a baking sheet lined with foil, spread the zucchini and squash cubes into a single layer. Roast the vegetables in the oven for 15–18 minutes or until the vegetables are soft and tender. Serve bite-size pieces to your child, cutting into smaller pieces if necessary.

Rosemary may help boost the immune system & improve blood circulation

STRAWBERRY BANANA
GREEK YOGURT

AGE 10 months plus
YIELD approximately ¾ cup
FOOD STORAGE refrigerator friendly
PREP TIME 5 minutes
COOK TIME no cook!

This recipe produces a simple, nutritious breakfast in about five minutes! You can occasionally substitute the strawberries for a different type of berry, such as blueberries, raspberries, or blackberries. This quantity makes enough for baby and parent. Alternatively, you can store the remaining yogurt in the refrigerator, and breakfast is conveniently ready for your baby tomorrow morning!

INGREDIENTS

- 2–3 medium whole strawberries, green tops removed
- ½ banana, peeled
- ½ cup plain Greek yogurt

1 Place the strawberries and banana in a blender. Add the minimum amount of water needed (try starting with ⅛ or ¼ cup) to puree the sauce to a smooth consistency. Taste the berry sauce. To adjust the flavors, add a little more banana if more sweetness is desired.

2 Transfer the berry sauce to a bowl and add the Greek yogurt. Mix well. Set aside a serving portion for your baby. The remaining portion is breakfast for you! Enjoy!

KHEEMA:
INDIAN GROUND BEEF

AGE 10 months plus
YIELD approximately 6 cups
FOOD STORAGE refrigerator friendly, freezer friendly
PREP TIME 5 minutes
COOK TIME 35 minutes

Kheema is a traditional South Asian medley of ground meat, potatoes, and peas. This recipe presents a milder version, specially designed for babies and toddlers, of a traditional kheema. Ground beef is an excellent source of protein and iron, and the sweet potato, peas, and spices add amazing nutrition. This is a wonderful one-pot meal! Try serving the kheema plain, with basmati rice, quinoa, or barley.

INGREDIENTS

- 2 tablespoons extra virgin olive oil
- ½ yellow onion, diced
- 1 teaspoon garlic, minced
- 1 teaspoon ginger, minced
- 1⅓ pounds ground beef, preferably organic, grass fed
- 1½ teaspoons kosher salt, divided (we recommend using salt only if your baby is 12 months plus)
- 2 teaspoons ground coriander
- 1 teaspoon ground cumin
- ½ teaspoon ground turmeric
- 2 cups sweet potatoes, diced into ½-inch-by-½-inch cubes
- 1 cup water
- 12-ounce package frozen peas, straight from freezer
- ¾ teaspoon black pepper
- 1 teaspoon fresh lime juice, seeds removed

1 Heat the oil in a medium saucepan over medium heat. Once hot, add the onions and sauté for 4–6 minutes or until soft and translucent. Add the garlic and ginger, and stir continuously for 30 seconds to prevent burning. Add the beef, break it into small pieces with the spoon, and allow it to brown for about 2 minutes. Add ½ teaspoon salt (if using), coriander, cumin, and turmeric. Mix well. Cook until the meat is brown and no longer pink, about 4–6 minutes.

2 Add the potatoes and the water. Mix well and cover with a tight-fitted lid. Cook for 12–15 minutes or until the potatoes are soft and tender, stirring occasionally. Add the frozen peas, remaining salt, pepper, and lime juice. Mix well and cook for 3–5 minutes or until the peas are soft enough for your baby.

3 Allow it to cool and serve, cutting into bite-size pieces appropriate for your baby. For adults and other family members who might enjoy a more flavorful, spicier version of this dish, try garnishing only the adult portions with freshly diced jalapeño pepper and/or freshly minced cilantro! Serve and enjoy!

Coriander may help digestion problems, such as upset stomach and gas.

MEDITERRANEAN COUSCOUS
WITH FETA, LEMON, & PARSLEY

AGE 10 months plus
YIELD approximately 5 cups
FOOD STORAGE refrigerator friendly
PREP TIME 8 minutes
COOK TIME 12 minutes

There's something so delicious about cool cucumber and creamy feta mixed with refreshing lemon juice! This recipe is a great one to try when your little one's palate is becoming more accustomed to lumpier textures, and it makes an excellent side dish for a family meal.

INGREDIENTS

- 1¼ cups water
- 1 medium-size cucumber
- Juice of 1 lemon, seeds removed
- 2 tablespoons extra virgin olive oil
- 1 garlic clove, finely minced
- 2 tablespoons fresh parsley, finely minced
- ½ teaspoon fresh ground pepper
- ⅔ cup feta cheese, crumbled
- 1¼ cups plain couscous, preferably organic

Parsley may stimulate the appetite and improve digestion.

1 Bring the water to a boil in a large saucepan.

2 In the meantime, cut the cucumber in half lengthwise, and scrape the seeds out with your finger or a spoon. Grate the cucumber (skin included), and place it in a large mixing bowl. Add the lemon juice, oil, garlic, parsley, pepper, and feta. When the water has reached a boil, add the couscous, and remove it from the heat immediately. Cover with a lid and allow it to rest for 5 minutes. Remove the lid and fluff the couscous with a fork.

3 Once the couscous has cooled slightly, add it to the bowl and mix well. You can spoon-feed this to your baby or, if she is old enough, let her dig in with a spoon of her own!

WARM LENTILS WITH
CUMIN AND CORIANDER

AGE 10 months plus
YIELD approximately 6 cups
FOOD STORAGE refrigerator friendly, freezer friendly
PREP TIME 5 minutes
COOK TIME 45 minutes

This hearty soup is truly a delight for the whole family. Lentils are a rich source of dietary fiber, iron, and protein. Try serving this healthy one-pot wonder on a cool fall or winter day for warmth and comfort! This recipe purposely makes a large batch so that the family can also enjoy it, or you can alternatively store in small, airtight containers, freeze, and have food ready for your baby when you need it!

INGREDIENTS

- 2 tablespoons extra virgin olive oil
- 2 cups yellow onion, diced
- 1 cup carrots, sliced
- 1 teaspoon fresh garlic, minced
- 2 cups small whole green lentils
- 6 cups low sodium vegetable broth, preferably organic
- 1½ teaspoons ground cumin
- 2 teaspoons ground coriander
- 1½ teaspoons kosher salt (optional: we recommend adding salt only for babies 12 months plus)
- ½ teaspoon black pepper
- 2 cups organic baby spinach, finely chopped
- 2 tablespoons freshly squeezed lemon juice, seeds removed

1 Heat the oil in a medium saucepan over medium heat. Once hot, add the onions and sauté for 4–6 minutes or until soft and translucent. Add the carrots and continue sautéing for another 4–5 minutes. Add the garlic and stir continuously for 30 seconds to prevent burning. Add the lentils, broth, cumin, coriander, salt (if using), and pepper. Mix well and bring the soup to a boil. Once boiling, reduce the heat to medium low, and cover with a tight-fitted lid. Simmer, stirring occasionally, for about 30 minutes or until the lentils and vegetables are soft and fully cooked.

2 Add the spinach and lemon juice and stir. Cook for an additional 2 minutes or until the spinach is tender. Serve to your child, cutting the vegetables into smaller pieces if necessary. Adults looking for a more flavorful version can add freshly diced jalapeño peppers and freshly minced cilantro to the adult portion only. To serve leftovers, add a small amount of water, mix well, reheat, and serve.

Cumin is a good source of iron and has infection-fighting properties.

DANCE PARTY
CHICKEN NUGGETS

AGE 10 months plus

YIELD approximately 60-80 nuggets

FOOD STORAGE refrigerator friendly, freezer friendly

PREP TIME 25 minutes

COOK TIME 15 minutes

Who doesn't love chicken nuggets?! We know we do, and we wanted a healthier take on this traditional American food. Not only will you have a dance party in your kitchen as you "shake it up" to bread the nuggets, but you'll have plenty left over to freeze, as this recipe makes a nice, large batch! Lightly breaded and baked, these tender nuggets are sure to have your baby begging for more. Try serving them with your child's favorite dipping sauce, such as ketchup, honey mustard, or barbeque sauce!

INGREDIENTS

- 1½ cups Italian-style bread crumbs
- 3 teaspoons fresh oregano, finely chopped (can substitute 1½ teaspoons dried oregano)

- 2 teaspoons garlic powder
- ½ teaspoon fresh ground black pepper
- ½ cup finely grated cheese, such as Pecorino Romano or Parmesan
- 3 eggs, preferably organic
- ½ cup milk, such as unsweetened almond milk or dairy milk
- 4 boneless, skinless chicken breasts (approximately 1½ pounds total weight), preferably organic, pounded to ½-inch thick and cut into "nugget-sized" pieces about 1 inch by 1 inch
- 2 tablespoons extra virgin olive oil, divided

Tip: Try using kitchen scissors to cut the chicken into nuggets!

Oregano is believed to be antibacterial, antiviral, & antifungal.

1 Preheat oven to 425 degrees.

2 Place the bread crumbs, oregano, garlic powder, pepper, and cheese into a large resealable plastic bag. Seal, and shake until everything is blended. (This is where the "dance party" comes in, so be sure to have your baby help you as you shake it up! Just make sure the bag is sealed tightly!)

3 Whisk the eggs and milk together in a large mixing bowl. Place all of the chicken nuggets into the bowl and stir with a spoon to ensure each piece gets coated with the egg mixture. Open the bag with the bread crumbs, and, using a slotted spoon, transfer the egg-coated nuggets from the bowl into the bag, allowing any excess egg mixture to drain first. Once all the chicken has been transferred, seal the bag, and—you guessed it—have another dance party! Shake it up thoroughly until each nugget is coated with bread crumbs. (There's nothing like dancing in the kitchen with your little one!)

4 Line a baking sheet with foil. Drizzle 1 tablespoon of the olive oil onto the foil and use a brush to spread an even coating. Add the nuggets to the baking sheet in a single layer (it's OK if the nuggets are close together, or you may use an additional baking sheet if you prefer), drizzle the other 1 tablespoon of oil loosely over the nuggets, and bake for 10–12 minutes, or until the bottom sides are golden brown. Flip each nugget, and bake for an additional 5 minutes. Allow to cool.

5 Once cool, serve these babies up with your little one's favorite sauce, such as ketchup, honey mustard, or barbeque sauce! This makes a big batch, so you can freeze whatever is left for a night you're in a hurry.

COCONUT CURRY GOAN FISH

AGE 10 months plus

YIELD 4 fish fillets

FOOD STORAGE refrigerator friendly for 1-2 days, freezer friendly

PREP TIME 13 minutes

COOK TIME 20 minutes

The Indian state of Goa is known for its beaches, and it overlooks the Arabian Sea. Warm flavors of coriander, cumin, turmeric, and coconut milk come together beautifully in this recipe. Fish is an excellent source of vitamins and nutrients, and it is an easy texture for a baby to handle, especially once it's mashed up and/or mixed with plain yogurt. Try serving this as a family dinner with a side of basmati rice or vegetables.

INGREDIENTS

- 2 tablespoons extra virgin olive oil
- 2 tablespoons green onion, finely minced
- 1½ teaspoons fresh garlic, finely minced

- 1 teaspoon fresh ginger, finely minced
- ½ teaspoon ground turmeric
- 1 teaspoon ground coriander
- ½ teaspoon ground cumin
- 1 teaspoon kosher salt, divided (optional: we recommend adding salt only for babies 12 mo+)
- 1¼ cups light coconut milk, preferably organic
- 2 tablespoons organic apple cider vinegar with the "mother"
- 4 steelhead trout filets, about 6 ounces each*
- 1 tablespoon fresh cilantro, finely minced
- Juice of ½ lemon, for sprinkling
- Plain yogurt, preferably organic (optional)

1 In a large sauté pan, heat the oil over medium heat. Add the green onion, garlic, and ginger. Stir continuously for about 1 minute to prevent burning. Add the turmeric, coriander, cumin, and ¼ teaspoon salt (if using). Sauté, stirring continuously, for 1 minute. Add the coconut milk and vinegar. Stir well and simmer the mixture uncovered for approximately 5 minutes.

2 Season the fish with ¾ teaspoon salt and carefully add it to the pan. (If the fish has the skin on, add it skin side up, flesh side down in the pan.) Cover and cook for approximately 10 minutes or until the fish is fully cooked and the flesh flakes apart easily with a fork. (Take care not to overcook the fish, or the meat will become tough.) Remove the fish from the pan, sprinkle with cilantro, and squeeze fresh lemon juice to taste.

3 To serve to baby, mash or cut the fish into bite-size pieces appropriate for your child, and serve! If your baby seems hesitant at first, try mixing the fish with a little bit of plain yogurt or one of her favorite purees. Adults looking for additional flavor and spice can add freshly minced jalapeno to the adult portion only.

Note: You may try replacing steelhead trout with a different type of fish, such as salmon, perch, or whitefish, but cooking time may vary slightly based on the type and thickness of the fish. If you can only find fish with the skin on, ask your local market to remove it for time savings.

Ginger is an antioxidant & helps support the immune system

PENNE WITH PUMPKIN & SAGE

AGE 10 months plus
YIELD approximately 6-8 cups
FOOD STORAGE refrigerator friendly, freezer friendly
PREP TIME 7 minutes
COOK TIME 35 minutes

Our Penne with Pumpkin and Sage is a savory and seasonal spin on your usual pasta dish! It's a great way to offer a comfort food to your baby while sneaking in the health benefits of pumpkin and sage. The cinnamon and nutmeg add a tasty flavor, making this a dish enjoyable for the entire family.

We also love that the pasta requires only half of the batch of sauce, which means you can save the other half in the freezer for a future pasta dinner!

INGREDIENTS

- 1 pound whole wheat penne pasta
- 2 tablespoons extra virgin olive oil
- 3 shallots, minced
- 3 cloves garlic, minced
- 2 cups vegetable broth
- 15 ounces pumpkin puree, preferably organic
- ½ cup coconut milk
- 1 tablespoon ground cinnamon
- 2 teaspoons ground nutmeg
- ½ teaspoon salt (optional: we recommend using salt only if your baby is 12 months plus)
- ¼ teaspoon pepper
- 8 fresh sage leaves, finely chopped
- ¼ cup grated cheese, such as Parmesan or Pecorino Romano

Sage may help stomach pain, bloating, and gas.

1 FOR THE PENNE PASTA

Follow the instructions on the pasta package, and cook the penne 1 minute less than recommended on the cooking instructions. Drain the pasta.

2 FOR THE PUMPKIN SAUCE

Heat the oil in a large sauce pot over medium heat. Add the shallots and sauté until soft and translucent, about 3 minutes. Add the garlic and sauté for 30 seconds, stirring continuously to prevent burning. Add the vegetable broth, pumpkin puree, and coconut milk. Stir until blended and smooth. Add the cinnamon, nutmeg, salt, and pepper. Bring to a boil. Add the sage, reduce the heat, and simmer for 5 minutes. Remove from heat and fold in the grated cheese.

3

Place the cooked pasta in a large bowl, and pour ½ of the pumpkin sauce over the pasta. Top with extra grated cheese, if desired, and toss well. Cut the pasta into bite-size pieces appropriate for your baby, and serve! Once the remaining pumpkin sauce is cooled, store it in an airtight container in the freezer for future use.

Note: Adults looking for extra spice and flavor may opt to add 1 teaspoon of Tabasco sauce to the adult portion only for a delicious kick!

TEMPEH FINGERS WITH
EASY TZATZIKI

AGE 10 months plus
YIELD approximately 24 pieces of tempeh
FOOD STORAGE refrigerator friendly
PREP TIME 25 minutes
COOK TIME 25 minutes

We love this recipe because it's a powerhouse of nutrition from top to bottom. The main player in this dish is the tempeh, and if you've never cooked with it before, we believe you'll find it so easy and tasty that this meal may become a weekly staple! Tempeh is an ancient food that is fermented, high in protein, low in sodium, and a great source of iron. It is made from soybeans.

In the marinade, we use coconut aminos, which contain an abundant source of 17 amino acids, minerals, and vitamins! The tempeh is served with a probiotic-packed Greek yogurt dipping sauce that is sure to encourage your little eater to "dippy dip!"

INGREDIENTS

FOR THE TEMPEH

- 4 tablespoons extra virgin olive oil
- 2 teaspoons liquid coconut aminos
- Squeeze of ½ a lemon, seeds removed
- 1 garlic clove, minced
- 1 teaspoon fresh oregano (can replace with ½ teaspoon dried oregano)
- ¼ teaspoon fresh ground black pepper
- 8 ounces tempeh, sliced horizontally into "fingers" about ¼-inch thick

FOR THE YOGURT SAUCE

- 1 cup Greek yogurt
- ½ teaspoon fresh dill (can replace with ¼ teaspoon dried dill weed)

Oregano is believed to be antibacterial, antiviral, & antifungal.

1 Preheat the oven to 350 degrees.

2 Combine the oil, coconut aminos, lemon juice, garlic, oregano, and pepper in a medium-sized bowl, and stir to combine. Add tempeh slices to the bowl, and gently mix with a spoon to coat all the pieces with the liquid. Marinate for 20 minutes.

3 Place yogurt and dill in a small bowl, and mix to combine.

4 Once marinated, arrange tempeh fingers in a single layer on a nonstick baking sheet, and bake for 12-15 minutes, or until the bottom side is lightly browned. Then gently turn each piece of tempeh over using a fork or pair of tongs, and bake for an additional 7–10 minutes or until the second side is lightly browned. Remove the tempeh from the oven and allow it to cool slightly so the pieces can be handled yet are still warm. (These can be served once fully cooled as well, if you prefer; no need to reheat leftovers tomorrow!)

5 Serve to baby, and let her dip the tempeh fingers into the yogurt sauce! Try serving this with a diced tomato and cucumber salad drizzled with balsamic vinegar.

Note: You can find both tempeh and coconut aminos in health food stores, and on Amazon. You may also substitute coconut aminos with low-sodium soy sauce.

BABY GAZPACHO

AGE 10 months plus

YIELD approximately 2½ cups

FOOD STORAGE refrigerator friendly, freezer friendly

PREP TIME approximately 6 minutes

COOK TIME no cook!

Gazpacho is a Spanish soup traditionally enjoyed in Andalucía and Portugal. It's packed with many fresh vegetables, and you don't even have to cook anything! Just toss all the ingredients in a blender and puree. It doesn't get any better than that! Gazpacho soup is traditionally served cold, but your baby may prefer it at room temperature.

INGREDIENTS

- 2 tomatoes, quartered
- 1 medium-size cucumber, roughly chopped
- ¼ cup yellow onion, roughly chopped
- ¼ cup green bell pepper, roughly chopped
- 2 tablespoons extra virgin olive oil
- 1 cup low-sodium vegetable juice, such as V8
- 1½ tablespoons distilled white vinegar
- ½ teaspoon kosher salt (optional: we recommend adding salt only for babies 12 months plus)
- ¼ teaspoon black pepper
- ¼ teaspoon garlic salt

1 Add all ingredients to the blender. Puree just until the ingredients are smooth and combined, taking care not to overmix. Serve cold or at room temperature.

Note: Adults looking for additional flavor and heat can add a few drops of Tabasco sauce to the adult portion only. Enjoy this meal with crackers or fresh, hot bread!

Pepper may help fight germs & increase the flow of digestive juices in the stomach.

SAMPLE FOOD SCHEDULE
FOR 12-MONTH-OLD-TODDLER

The following feeding schedule is a sample of what one mom feeds her 12-month-old toddler. This is simply one example that is intended to act as a guide only. All babies have different feeding times and eat different quantities. We recommend that you consult your pediatrician with any questions or concerns with regards to feeding your baby.

If a food name is italicized, that means you'll find the recipe in this book.

7:00 A.M. (BREAKFAST):
1 serving breakfast food, such as 1 *Poached Egg*
1 serving fruit, such as 2–3 diced strawberries or diced apple
Breast milk or dairy milk in a sippy cup (drink to thirst)

10:00 A.M. (SNACK):
Diced fruit, such as ½ kiwi or ½ avocado
Breast milk or dairy milk in a sippy cup (drink to thirst)

1:00 P.M. (LUNCH):
1 serving lunch food (about ½ a sandwich), such as *Cool Cucumber Sandwich Bites*
1 serving vegetable, such as *Please More Peas*
Breast milk or dairy milk in a sippy cup (drink to thirst)

4:00 P.M. (SNACK):
Almond Butter Banana Boat or cheese with diced fruit
Breast milk or dairy milk in a sippy cup (drink to thirst)

6:00 P.M. (DINNER):
2–3 ounces meat or protein, such as *Turkey Cutlets*
1 serving vegetable (preferably a different color than lunch), such as diced bell pepper, tomato, or *Butternut Squash with Rosemary and Sage*
Breast milk or dairy milk in a sippy cup (drink to thirst)

Tip: Try feeding your child a "rainbow" of solid foods throughout the day so that she gets a variety of nutrition. For example, if you serve something green for lunch, try serving something yellow for a snack, something orange for dinner, etc. To maintain a balanced diet, try feeding your child a fruit, a vegetable, a protein, and a grain through the course of the day.

12 MONTHS PLUS:
MILESTONES & NEW INGREDIENTS

This is a milestone stage because now children can begin to eat even more of what the family enjoys, which makes the entire cooking process easier and more streamlined! Foods that we worried about for our little ones—such as salt and honey—are now OK for them to indulge in (introduced slowly and in moderation, of course).

Your toddler will have favorite foods, there is no question about that, and he will also have foods that he may refuse. And you want him to eat, of course! This is why it's common in this stage to fall into a "food rut," otherwise known as serving the same thing over and over to ensure your child will eat something. If you find yourself stuck in food rut, refer to our "Helpful Tips" chapter on some ways to remedy this issue.

The main points to remember in this stage are:

- KEEP FOOD AND QUANTITIES SMALL. While your baby's palate is becoming more advanced, he still needs his food cut up into small bites to avoid any potential choking hazards. Large quantities of food may be overwhelming to him, so serve small quantities of food at a time, and give more as needed.
- WATCH OUT FOR FOOD RUTS. Don't deprive your child of his or her favorites, but make sure you are still providing other options to try. (See "Helpful Tips" chapter for more information on this issue.)
- FOLLOW THE "THREE SECTION" RULE. We recommend purchasing a plate that has three sections (available at most baby stores). We have lived by this rule for our toddlers and have had great success. Here's how you do it: provide your toddler a sectioned plate with three different foods in small quantities. Ensure that at least one food is something that you know your toddler will eat and enjoy. For example, if your toddler loves strawberries, fill a three-sectioned plate with a few small pieces of chicken, broccoli, and strawberries. Encourage your child to try all three foods.
- NO COOKING OR PREPARING NEW MEALS. While this one may sound hard to follow, it's important. Babies as little as 1-year-old catch on to the fact that you will become a "short-order cook" until they get what they want, and this can quickly become a habit. Stop it before it starts! And remember, it is perfectly OK if your baby doesn't eat a full dinner. He will eat again tomorrow. If you have any ongoing concerns, be sure to speak to your pediatrician.
- TRY, TRY AGAIN. If you give your baby/toddler broccoli once or twice and he refuses it, don't assume that he doesn't like it altogether. If he doesn't like broccoli sautéed the way you prepared it, he may like it baked, blanched, or prepared another way. Try to keep an open mind, and refrain from jumping to conclusions too quickly. Your persistence will pay off in the long run, and you will successfully create a good eater!

Look for the following icons on each recipe to determine how it can be served:

 PUREE

 MASHED

 SPOON FEED

 SELF FEED

 FAMILY FRIENDLY

COOL CUCUMBER
SANDWICH BITES

AGE 12 months plus
YIELD 1 sandwich
FOOD STORAGE refrigerator friendly
PREP TIME 5 minutes
COOK TIME no cook!

These mini sandwich bites are not only refreshing on a hot summer's day, but also a healthy option to take on the go. They're an excellent finger food for baby and something the whole family can enjoy—When Ali makes this for her daughter, Penelope, she always makes one for herself too! Serve this up with a side of diced fruit, such as mango or melon, for a delicious summer lunch. These sandwiches can be made ahead of time and stored in the refrigerator.

INGREDIENTS

- 1–1½ tablespoons cream cheese (enough to spread a thin layer), softened
- 1 slice whole wheat bread
- 2 tablespoons grated cucumber (about ⅓ cucumber), peeling skin is optional
- ½ teaspoon fresh dill, minced

1 Spread the cream cheese onto the slice of bread in a thin layer. Cut bread evenly in half. Pat the grated cucumber dry with a paper towel to remove excess moisture. Top one half of the bread with grated cucumber, followed by dill.

2 Place the other half on top to make a sandwich. (Be sure to give it a good press so that the halves stick together!) Cut the sandwich into bite-size pieces appropriate for your child. Serve!

Dill is used to aid digestion problems and intestinal gas.

5 O'CLOCK PASTA

AGE 12 months plus
YIELD approximately 8-9 cups
FOOD STORAGE refrigerator friendly, freezer friendly
PREP TIME 6 minutes
COOK TIME 12 minutes

This dish was inspired by Ina Garten's Midnight Spaghetti; it's a meal she says is a go-to for chefs at the end of a late-night shift because they are starving and it's so easy to whip up! For us, it became our healthy, baby-friendly version of mac-'n'-cheese. But thankfully we aren't cooking it at midnight, we're making it at 5 o'clock! This is a guilty pleasure, make-in-a-hurry meal that your little one will love—and so will you. We couldn't stop laughing at how crazy our little kids and their friends went for their 5 O'clock Pasta!

INGREDIENTS

- 1 pound whole wheat organic pasta (preferably something easy for little fingers to grab, such as fusilli)
- ⅓ cup extra virgin olive oil
- 4 cloves of garlic, minced
- 5 tablespoons goat cheese
- 2 teaspoons fresh thyme (1 teaspoon dried will work in a pinch)
- 2 teaspoons fresh oregano (1 teaspoon dried will work in a pinch)
- 1 teaspoon kosher salt
- 1 tablespoon fresh squeezed lemon juice (from about ½ lemon)

1 Boil the water in a medium saucepan, and cook the pasta according to the instructions on the package. When draining the pasta, reserve 1½ cups of the pasta water and set it aside.

2 Once the pasta is cooked, heat the oil in a larger saucepan over medium heat. Sauté the garlic for 30 seconds or until fragrant, stirring continuously to prevent burning. Add the reserved pasta water and bring to a boil.

3 Once the amount of water is reduced to about ⅓ (about 5 minutes), add the drained pasta to the pot and toss. Remove from the heat, and mix in the goat cheese, herbs, salt, and lemon juice until the goat cheese is melted and evenly distributed. Once cool enough, serve to baby, cutting into bite-size pieces appropriate for your child. This is a great finger food for little hands! For adults looking for extra flavor and spice, try adding crushed red pepper flakes to the adult portion only.

Garlic is used to build the immune system.

POACHED EGGS

AGE 12 months plus
YIELD 2 eggs
FOOD STORAGE refrigerator friendly
PREP TIME 1 minute
COOK TIME 9 minutes

This recipe is a staple in Amy's house. Oftentimes, we're so busy caring for our kids that we put our own nutrition on the back burner. This recipe is designed to feed you and your baby simultaneously. The texture of a poached egg is soft and easy for a baby to eat, and it's a welcomed change from the standard scrambled or fried egg!

From a nutritional standpoint, eggs are a great source of nutrients for both you and your child. Eggs contain lots of protein and are chock-full of B vitamins and brain-boosting choline. And they are supereasy to prepare!

INGREDIENTS

- 1 teaspoon unsalted butter
- ⅓ cup water
- 2 eggs, preferably organic
- Small pinch kosher salt
- Small pinch black pepper

1 In a medium-size skillet, melt the butter over medium heat, and distribute it evenly across the pan to prevent sticking. Once melted, immediately add the water. When the pan begins to steam, crack each egg into the skillet side by side, aiming for the yolks to be centered.

2 Lightly season the eggs with salt and pepper. Cover the pan with a lid, and reduce the heat to medium low. Cook the eggs for approximately 5–7 minutes or until the yolks are hard and fully cooked. Serve 1 egg to your baby, mashing or cutting into bite-size pieces appropriate for your child. The other egg is for you! Enjoy!

Pepper may help fight germs & increase the flow of digestive juices in the stomach.

BASIL AND KALE FRITTATA

AGE 12 months plus
YIELD 1 frittata
FOOD STORAGE refrigerator friendly
PREP TIME 6 minutes
COOK TIME 18 minutes

The best part about this recipe is the incredible versatility it offers: frittatas can be eaten for breakfast, lunch, or dinner; they can be served hot or cold; and you can easily substitute the vegetables. Do you have a bell pepper that needs to be used within the next day or two? Add it in! Not crazy about kale? Try replacing it with fresh baby spinach. This recipe is designed to create one meal that feeds the entire family quickly and easily, and your blender does all the work!

INGREDIENTS

- 6 organic eggs, cracked
- ½ cup organic milk
- 7–8 fresh, medium-size basil leaves
- 1 cup organic kale leaves (large stems removed), tightly packed
- ¼ cup ricotta cheese
- ¼ teaspoon baking powder
- ½ teaspoon kosher salt
- ¼ teaspoon black pepper
- ½ teaspoon unsalted butter, for greasing
- ½ cup shredded cheddar cheese or gruyere cheese, divided

Basil is a powerful antioxidant with antibacterial properties.

1 Preheat the oven to 375 degrees.

2 Add the eggs, milk, basil, kale, ricotta, baking powder, salt, and pepper to the blender. Pulse the blender approximately 10–15 times or just until the basil and kale leaves are chopped into small pieces. Do not overmix or turn the blender on continuously.

3 Place a nonstick skillet over medium-low heat. Grease the bottom and sides of the pan thoroughly with butter to prevent sticking. Once the skillet is warm, pour the contents of the blender into the skillet. Add ¼ cup cheese evenly over the mixture. Cover with a tight-fitted lid and cook for approximately 7–8 minutes or until the majority of the egg mixture is solidified. (Tilt the pan to test the consistency of the egg.)

4 Add the remaining ¼ cup cheese evenly over the top of the frittata. Transfer the skillet from the stove to the oven, and bake uncovered for 5–7 minutes or until the egg mixture is completely solidified and the cheese has melted.

5 Allow the frittata to slightly cool in the skillet. Using a spatula, gently loosen the edges of the frittata and transfer it to a cutting board. Slice the frittata into wedges using a knife or pizza cutter. Serve!

BABY CAPRESE SALAD

AGE 12 months plus
YIELD 1½ cups
FOOD STORAGE refrigerator friendly
PREP TIME 7 minutes
COOK TIME no cook!

If you're looking for a healthy, no-cook recipe, caprese salad is a great option! The key to making this salad delicious is the quality of the ingredients you choose. Try using tomatoes from your garden, the farmers' market, or a local farm share while they're in season. This recipe also doubles well, so you can make it in bulk and store it in the refrigerator for a few days. Try making this for a healthy afternoon snack!

INGREDIENTS

- 1 cup tomatoes (preferably heirloom, yellow tomatoes, cherry tomatoes, or a combination), diced into ½-inch-by-½-inch pieces
- ½ cup mozzarella, diced into ½-inch-by-½-inch cubes
- 1 teaspoon fresh basil, finely minced
- ¼ teaspoon balsamic vinegar
- Freshly ground pepper

1 Place the tomatoes, mozzarella, basil, and balsamic vinegar in a small bowl. Mix the ingredients well. Lightly season the salad with freshly ground pepper. Serve bite-sized pieces to your child, cutting into smaller pieces if needed.

Basil is a powerful antioxidant with antibacterial properties.

CHICKEN TIKKA MASALA

AGE 12 months plus
YIELD approximately 4 cups
FOOD STORAGE refrigerator friendly, freezer friendly
PREP TIME 12 minutes
COOK TIME 25 minutes

This Indian dish is an American favorite! This recipe is inspired by Amy's aunt Zarina, who makes Indian dishes approachable and delicious. Bite-size pieces of chicken swimming in a warm, creamy tomato sauce is something the whole family will enjoy! This is a wonderful, one-pot, no-fuss weeknight meal. Chicken Tikka Masala is traditionally served with basmati rice and/or naan bread, but if you're looking for a healthier spin, try it with brown rice or bulgur.

INGREDIENTS

- 2 tablespoons extra virgin olive oil
- 1 medium yellow onion, finely diced
- ¾ teaspoon garlic paste
- ¼ teaspoon ginger paste
- 1 teaspoon ground coriander
- ¼ teaspoon ground cinnamon
- ¼ teaspoon ground clove
- 2 teaspoons tandoori masala (spice mixture purchased from Indian grocery or ethnic food market)
- 1 pound organic boneless, skinless chicken breast, cut into ½-inch-by-½-inch cubes
- 1 teaspoon kosher salt
- 15 ounces tomato sauce, no sodium added
- 1¼ cups half-and-half, preferably organic
- *Optional: fresh cilantro, finely minced for garnish

1 Heat the oil in a large saucepan over medium-high heat. Add the onions and fry until they are lightly browned, about 5–8 minutes. Reduce the heat to medium and add the garlic and ginger pastes. Stir continuously for 30 seconds to prevent burning. Add the coriander, cinnamon, clove, and tandoori masala, and cook for approximately 2 minutes, stirring frequently.

2 Add the chicken and salt, and stir to incorporate the spices. Cook the chicken for 4–5 minutes uncovered, stirring occasionally. Cover the pan with a tight-fitted lid and continue cooking for another 4–5 minutes or until the chicken is fully cooked and no longer pink in the center. Slowly add the tomato sauce and half-and-half, and stir to combine well. Cook for 1–2 minutes.

3 Remove from the heat and garnish with fresh cilantro if desired. Allow the chicken to cool, remove your baby's portion, and spoon-feed or serve bite-size pieces appropriate for your child. For adults looking to add more flavor and spice, you can optionally add freshly minced green chilies to the adult portion only.

Coriander may help digestion problems, such as upset stomach and gas.

BABY BEEF AND GREENS

AGE 12 months plus
YIELD approximately 9 cups
FOOD STORAGE refrigerator friendly, freezer friendly
PREP TIME 8 minutes
COOK TIME 25 minutes

When we are looking to get dinner on the table in about 30 minutes, this is a meal we often turn to. It contains a protein, complex carbohydrate, and vegetable all in one pot! It's a delicious meal the entire family can enjoy. Since it makes a large portion, store the rest in an airtight container, refrigerate or freeze, and you'll have a dinner ready for another night of the week!

INGREDIENTS

- 2 tablespoons extra virgin olive oil
- ½ yellow onion, diced
- 2 cloves garlic, minced
- 1⅓ pounds ground beef, preferably organic
- 2 cups dry, whole wheat fusilli pasta
- 2 teaspoons kosher salt
- 1 teaspoon black pepper
- 2 tablespoons fresh sage leaves, minced
- 2 teaspoons dried oregano
- 1 Yukon gold potato, diced
- 1 cup organic, low-sodium vegetable broth
- 2½ cups organic baby spinach, tightly packed
- Freshly grated Parmesan cheese or Pecorino Romano, for garnishing

Sage may help stomach pain, bloating, and gas.

1 Heat the oil in a large saucepan over medium heat. Once the oil is hot, add the onions and sauté for 4–5 minutes or until soft and translucent. Add the garlic and cook for another 30 seconds, stirring frequently to prevent burning. Add the ground beef and brown, stirring occasionally, for about 5–7 minutes.

2 In the meantime, bring a medium-sized pot of salted water to a boil. Once boiling, add the pasta and cook according to the package instructions. Strain the pasta, reserving 1 cup of pasta cooking water. Set aside.

3 Once the ground beef is browned, add salt, pepper, sage, oregano, potatoes, and vegetable broth. Stir well to combine the ingredients, and bring to a boil. Reduce the heat to medium low and simmer for 7–10 minutes, stirring occasionally. Once the meat is fully cooked and the potatoes are tender, add the spinach. Cook for 1–2 minutes or until the spinach wilts. Add the fusilli pasta and reserved pasta water to the meat. Toss well to combine, taste, and adjust seasonings if needed. Garnish with freshly grated Parmesan or Pecorino Romano cheese. Serve, cutting into bite-size pieces for your baby if needed.

PARSI RAVA: AN INDIAN
SPIN ON CREAM OF WHEAT

AGE 12 months plus

YIELD 1½ cups

FOOD STORAGE refrigerator friendly

PREP TIME 4 minutes

COOK TIME 13 minutes

Parsi rava is an Indian breakfast food traditionally made from semolina (wheat flour). This dish whips up a bowl of breakfast similar to a warm, winter pudding with pleasing hints of cardamom and nutmeg. Try serving it for breakfast—or even dessert—on a cool fall or winter day! The whole milk aids in a nice calcium boost for your toddler. This recipe doubles well, so if your baby enjoys it, make twice as much next time, and breakfast is ready for several days!

INGREDIENTS

- 1 tablespoon unsalted butter
- ⅓ cup Cream of Wheat
- ¼ teaspoon kosher salt
- ¼ teaspoon ground cardamom
- ¼ teaspoon ground nutmeg
- 2½ cups whole milk, preferably organic
- 1 teaspoon local honey

Cardamom may help ease stomach & intestinal gas

1 Melt the butter in a medium saucepan over medium heat. Add the Cream of Wheat, and toast for about 2 minutes.

2 Add the salt, cardamom, and nutmeg. Stir and toast for 1 minute. Remove the pan from the heat, and slowly add the milk while stirring.

3 Return the pan to the heat. Bring the milk to a low boil, then reduce the heat and simmer for 3–5 minutes, stirring frequently to prevent the milk from burning. Add the honey and stir to combine well.

4 The consistency of the rava should be similar to rice pudding. It will thicken over time, so, if needed, add a small amount of milk, stir, and reheat if serving leftovers. This dish can be served cold or warm.

SCARBOROUGH FAIR
GRILLED CHEESE

AGE 12 months plus
YIELD 1 full sandwich for parent, ½ sandwich for baby
FOOD STORAGE best served immediately
PREP TIME 7 minutes
COOK TIME 13 minutes

During one of our combined work sessions for this cookbook (and playdates with our little ones), we became very hungry! Ironically, two moms writing a cookbook found themselves stumped on what to make for lunch. Ali had these ingredients on hand, and we got creative. We call it Scarborough Fair Grilled Cheese named after the Simon and Garfunkel song, where they sing of "parsley, sage, rosemary, and thyme."

INGREDIENTS

- 3 slices whole wheat bread
- 1½ tablespoons whole milk ricotta cheese
- 1½ tablespoons goat cheese
- ¾ teaspoon fresh parsley, finely chopped
- ¾ teaspoon fresh sage, finely chopped
- ¾ teaspoon fresh rosemary, finely chopped
- ¾ teaspoon fresh thyme, finely chopped
- 1½ slices American cheese
- 1 tablespoon butter, divided

1 Lay out all 3 pieces of bread and slice 1 in half. Set aside.

2 Combine ricotta cheese, goat cheese, and fresh herbs in a small bowl, and mix thoroughly. Spread 2 tablespoons of the cheese mixture onto 1 full slice of bread, top with 1 slice of American cheese, and place the other slice of bread on top to make a sandwich. Repeat this process with the remaining tablespoon of cheese mixture, ½ slice of American cheese, and the 2 halves of the remaining bread slice (which will be baby's portion).

3 Place a medium frying pan on the stove over medium heat. Melt ½ tablespoon of butter in the pan, and place the sandwiches into the pan. Allow both sandwiches to cook on one side until golden brown, about 5 minutes.

4 Melt the remaining ½ tablespoon butter in the pan, and immediately flip the sandwiches. Cook until the second side becomes golden-brown, about 2–4 minutes. Remove from the heat. When the sandwiches are cool enough to handle, cut baby's sandwich into bite-size squares and serve.

Parsley may stimulate the appetite and improve digestion.

TURKEY CUTLETS

AGE 12 months plus
YIELD approximately 10-14 cutlets
FOOD STORAGE refrigerator friendly, freezer friendly
PREP TIME 9 minutes
COOK TIME 18 minutes

Amy's grandmother, a renowned caterer, cooked hundreds of cutlets at a time for her family while they were growing up. She and her three sisters would devour them in a matter of days, and, once again, they'd be left cutletless.

These little patties appease children of all ages, from babies to teenagers. They refrigerate and freeze well, making for an ideal leftover choice when you're in a pinch. Try serving these plain, with mashed avocado, ketchup, hummus, sour cream, or your baby's favorite dipping sauce, and show them how to dip! If at first your baby seems reluctant, you can try melting some cheese on top. Adults can also try these cutlets in slider form with mustard or ketchup, or crumbled over a salad.

INGREDIENTS

- 1⅓ pounds ground turkey, preferably organic
- ¾ teaspoon kosher salt
- ½ teaspoon black pepper
- ½ teaspoon ground cumin
- 1 teaspoon ground coriander
- ½ teaspoon ground turmeric
- 2 teaspoons garlic paste
- 1 tablespoon fresh lemon juice, seeds removed
- 1 egg, lightly beaten
- 2 tablespoons extra virgin olive oil, divided

The chemicals in turmeric may decrease inflammation.

1 Place the turkey, salt, pepper, cumin, coriander, turmeric, garlic paste, lemon juice, and egg in a large mixing bowl. Mix the ingredients thoroughly with your hands.

2 Create small hamburger patties, or "sliders," 2½ inches wide and no taller than ½ inch to ensure they cook through. Set the cutlets aside on a plate.

3 Heat 1 tablespoon of oil in a large sauté pan over medium heat. Once the oil is hot, pan fry the cutlets in batches, placing 5–6 patties in the pan at a time. Take care not to overcrowd the pan or flatten the patties by pressing down with the spatula. Cook the cutlets for 3–5 minutes on each side or until the patties are golden brown on both sides, fully cooked, and no longer pink in the center.

4 Transfer the cooked cutlets to a plate lined with a paper towel to drain any excess oil. Add the remaining 1 tablespoon of oil, pan fry the next batch, and repeat the process. Allow them to cool, and serve bite-size pieces appropriate for your child.

SPINACH AND GOAT CHEESE
MINI MUFFINS

AGE 12 months plus
YIELD 36 mini muffins
FOOD STORAGE refrigerator friendly, freezer friendly
PREP TIME 12 minutes
COOK TIME 30 minutes

These mini spinach and goat cheese muffins are absolutely awesome! Once completed, you'll have 36 delicious snack-size mini muffins, and an amazing-smelling kitchen! These are a staple in our home. We keep these in a plastic sealed bag in our freezers for snack time in a pinch, and we can almost never refrain from snacking on one of these ourselves! To defrost, simply microwave for 10–20 seconds. It is important to use mini-muffin tins (as opposed to a regular muffin tin) for this recipe, considering the size of the bites and the cook time.

INGREDIENTS

- 3 tablespoons unsalted butter, divided
- 2 shallots, minced
- 1 garlic clove, minced
- 1 (16-ounce) package of frozen spinach, straight from freezer
- ½ cup water
- 2 eggs
- 1 cup goat cheese, crumbled or creamy
- ½ cup ricotta cheese
- ½ cup grated Pecorino Romano
- ½ teaspoon pepper
- 1 teaspoon fresh thyme
- 1 teaspoon ground nutmeg

Thyme contains chemicals that may help bacterial and fungal infections.

1 Preheat the oven to 350 degrees.

2 In a large skillet, melt 2 tablespoons of butter over medium heat. Add shallots and sauté until soft and translucent, about 3–5 minutes. Add garlic and sauté for 1 minute, stirring continuously to prevent burning. Add frozen spinach and water. Cook the spinach until thawed, stirring occasionally. Set aside.

3 In a medium-sized mixing bowl, whisk the eggs. Add the cheeses, pepper, thyme, and nutmeg. Add the spinach mixture to the bowl, stirring to combine until fully incorporated.

4 Grease your mini-muffin tins using the remaining 1 tablespoon of butter. Fill each muffin tin ¾ full of the mixture. Bake for 20–25 minutes or until the sides appear lightly browned.

5 Once cool, gently run a knife around the circumference of each muffin to loosen and remove it. If you have only 1 mini-muffin tin, repeat the process with the remaining mixture. To store, place them in small airtight containers and refrigerate or freeze.

THE ALMOND BUTTER
BANANA BOAT

AGE 12 months plus
YIELD 1 banana sandwich
FOOD STORAGE best if served immediately
PREP TIME 3 minutes
COOK TIME no cook!

When time and energy are scarce, this is a go-to snack. Our kids absolutely love the banana boat, and it is so filling and satisfying, we typically make an extra one for ourselves! We have fun eating this one together, and smiles and giggles fill our kitchens! Be sure to offer your tot plenty of milk or water between bites of this delicious, gooey snack.

INGREDIENTS

- 1 banana, peeled
- 1 teaspoon creamy, unsalted, organic almond butter

1 Cut the banana in half. Slice both halves of the banana lengthwise down the middle. Spread a thin layer of almond butter down the center of one half of the banana. Place the other half on top to create a banana sandwich. Repeat with the other half.

2 Chop the banana sandwich into bite-size chunks appropriate for your child. Serve and enjoy!

MINI BASIL MEAT LOAVES

AGE 12 months plus
YIELD 12 miniature meat loaves
FOOD STORAGE refrigerator friendly, freezer friendly
PREP TIME 18 minutes
COOK TIME 25 minutes

Allow your toddler an indulgent visit to the mouth-watering flavors of the Deep South! Your child will appreciate this comfort food, and you will appreciate having lunch or dinner ready made in your freezer! This recipe specially yields 12 miniature meat loaves, so you can freeze them and defrost as needed. Place two or three meat loaves at a time in a plastic bag, then place them in an airtight container and freeze. They're like the gift that keeps on giving!

"If you can stand the sticker shock, grass-fed beef does have advantages over grain-fed beef. Grass-fed beef is generally leaner with fewer calories per serving. The fats are healthier with a higher proportion of omega-3s. However, because it has less fat, grass-fed beef needs to be cooked and often requires less time in the oven than grain-fed beef. Also, grass-fed beef can have a darker color, as it has more beta carotene."—Dr. Elissa Levine, pediatrician.

INGREDIENTS

- ¼ tablespoon unsalted butter
- 1 egg, preferably organic
- 1⅓ pounds ground beef, preferably organic and/or grass-fed beef
- 1 teaspoon kosher salt
- ½ teaspoon black pepper
- 1 teaspoon dried oregano
- 1 tablespoon yellow mustard
- ½ cup panko bread crumbs
- ¼ yellow onion, whole
- 2 cloves garlic, whole
- ½ red bell pepper, seeds removed, roughly chopped
- 7 medium-size fresh basil leaves
- Approximately ¼ cup of water

Basil is a powerful antioxidant with antibacterial properties.

1 Preheat the oven to 350 degrees.

2 Thoroughly grease the bottom and sides of a muffin pan with butter to prevent sticking. In a medium-size mixing bowl, add the egg and lightly beat it with a fork. Add the beef, salt, pepper, oregano, mustard, and bread crumbs to the mixing bowl. Mix with clean hands to combine the mixture. Set aside.

3 In a blender, add the onion, garlic, bell pepper, basil leaves, and the minimum amount of water needed to puree (preferably not more than ¼ cup). Puree until smooth. Slowly add the puree to the meat. Thoroughly mix all the ingredients with your hands. Fill each of the 12 muffin containers to the top with the meat loaf mixture using an ice cream scoop. Then, use the back of the ice cream scoop to compress and even out the top of each mini meat loaf.

4 Bake for approximately 23–26 minutes or until the center of the mini meat loaves registers 160 degrees with a meat thermometer. Allow them to cool slightly, then gently run a knife along the circumference of each meat loaf to loosen it. Gently remove them from the pan, and serve bite-size pieces appropriate for your baby. You can also try serving these as mini meat loaf sliders between two whole wheat buns with ketchup or mustard. If at first your toddler seems hesitant, try melting a little cheese on top, or serve the meat loaf with your child's favorite dipping sauce, such as ketchup, honey mustard, or barbeque sauce.

SWEET POTATO GNOCCHI

AGE 12 months plus

YIELD approximately 6 cups (90-120 gnocchi total)

FOOD STORAGE refrigerator friendly, freezer friendly

TOTAL ACTIVE TIME (COOK & PREP): 55 minutes to make a batch, but only 10 minutes from frozen

This dish is one of our favorites! It's savory, nutritious, just the right amount of sweet, and our kids eat it like champs every time. We've also crafted this recipe to be both egg free and gluten free. One batch of this yields several servings. If you make it for your family, you'll have some left to freeze, and if you make it just for baby, well, then you'll really have some to freeze! Making homemade pasta is easier than you might think—and you don't need a fancy pasta maker!

INGREDIENTS

- 2 medium-size sweet potatoes (about 2 pounds)
- 3 cups gluten-free flour (we recommend Bob's Red Mill Gluten-Free Flour Blend), plus extra as needed
- 1 cup grated Pecorino Romano cheese (or grated Parmesan cheese), plus extra for topping
- 1 teaspoon grated nutmeg
- 1 teaspoon kosher salt
- 1 teaspoon fresh cracked black pepper

FOR THE BUTTER-SAGE SAUCE

- ¼ cup (½ stick) butter
- 1 tablespoon fresh sage leaves, chopped (approximately 8 leaves)

Sage may help stomach pain, bloating, and gas.

RECIPE CONTINUED...

SWEET POTATO GNOCCHI CONTINUED...

1 Preheat the oven to 400 degrees.

2 Scrub sweet potatoes clean, then pierce with a fork a few times all around. Place in oven directly on rack and bake until soft (about 50 minutes–1 hour).

3 While the potatoes are in the oven, place flour, cheese, nutmeg, salt, and pepper in a large bowl. Whisk until thoroughly combined. Set aside.

4 Once potatoes are out of the oven, slice open and allow to cool. Scoop out the flesh, place in a food processor, and puree until you reach a completely smooth consistency. (If you do not have a food processor you may use a high-powered blender. If necessary, add water one tablespoon at a time to achieve a smooth consistency. Take care not to add too much water.) Transfer the puree to a large bowl.

5 Add the flour mixture 1 cup at a time to the bowl with the sweet potatoes, blending using either a spatula or your hands. The mixture should slowly take on a doughy consistency; you will know it is ready once it forms into a large ball that is firm and moist, but does not stick to your fingers. (Add additional flour as necessary by the tablespoon until you reach the desired consistency.)

6 Transfer the dough to a clean surface lightly dusted with flour. Divide the dough into 6 smaller balls of approximately equal size. Using the palms of your hands, gently roll 1 of the dough balls back and forth until it takes on the shape of a long rope, about 16 inches long and ½ inch in diameter. Using a sharp knife, cut the rope into 1-inch pieces, and transfer to a plate. Repeat this process with the remaining 5 dough balls until all pieces are on the plate (you can use parchment paper and stack the gnocchi in layers). Place in the freezer to allow gnocchi to firm.

7 Fill a large pot with water (approximately 4 quarts) and bring to a boil over high heat. While you wait for the water to boil, prepare the Butter Sage Sauce (see below).

8 Once the water is boiling, lower the heat to medium and place the desired number of gnocchi in the pot (this recipe is based on approximately 42 pieces of gnocchi, which will feed 2 adults and 2 children), stirring gently with a wooden spoon to be sure they do not stick together. They are cooked when they begin to rise to the surface. They cook fast (only about 2 minutes!), so don't leave them unattended after you drop them into the water. Using a slotted spoon, remove the gnocchi from the water as they rise and place them directly into the pan with the butter-sage sauce. Stir to coat well.

9 Sprinkle lightly with Pecorino Romano cheese, cut baby's portion into appropriate bite-size pieces, and serve! You can freeze the remaining gnocchi in an airtight freezer bag for up to 6 months.

FOR THE BUTTER-SAGE SAUCE

1 Place the butter in a medium-size skillet over medium-high heat until golden-brown flecks appear (about 5–7 minutes). Remove from the heat and add sage leaves. (They should begin to turn crispy right away.) Stir and set aside.

Notes: An adult-size serving is approximately 1 cup, or 14 pieces of gnocchi; a toddler-size serving is approximately ½ cup, or 7 pieces of gnocchi. Once you already have a large batch in the freezer and need a fast dinner for your toddler, bring a small pot of water (approximately 4 cups) to a boil, and cook 7 or 8 pieces of gnocchi. You can make a fast butter sauce by simply microwaving 1 tablespoon of butter, adding a chopped sage leaf if desired, and tossing with the gnocchi. You can replace the gluten-free flour with regular or whole wheat flour if you prefer.

SAMPLE FOOD SCHEDULE
FOR 15-MONTH-OLD-TODDLER

The following feeding schedule is a sample of what one mom feeds her 15-month-old toddler. This is simply one example that is intended to act as a guide only. All children have different feeding times and eat different quantities. We recommend that you consult your pediatrician with any questions or concerns with regards to feeding your child.

At this stage your child may still be breastfeeding or may be drinking cow's milk or another milk choice, such as unsweetened almond milk. Consult your child's pediatrician regarding milk choices for your child.

If a food name is italicized, that means you'll find the recipe in this book.

7:00 A.M. (BREAKFAST):	1 serving breakfast food, such as *Strawberry Ricotta Toast* or *Sow Your Oats?* 1 serving fruit, such as blueberries or diced cantaloupe Breast milk or dairy milk in a sippy cup (drink to thirst)
10:00 A.M. (SNACK):	Diced fruit, such as apple or orange, and diced cheese Breast milk or dairy milk in a sippy cup (drink to thirst)
1:00 P.M. (LUNCH):	1 serving lunch food, such as *The Avocado, Tomato, Hummus Sandwich* 1 vegetable, such as diced bell pepper or *Okra Wheels with Turmeric* Breast milk or dairy milk in a sippy cup (drink to thirst)
4:00 P.M. (SNACK):	Diced vegetables, such as *Kiddie Crudite* or *Krispy Kale Chips* Breast milk or dairy milk in a sippy cup (drink to thirst)
6:00 P.M. (DINNER):	2–3 ounces meat or protein, such as *Slow Cooker Chicken Tacos* or *Chana Masala* 1 serving vegetable (preferably a different color than previous meal), such as diced bell pepper, tomato, or *Butternut Squash with Rosemary and Sage* Breast milk or dairy milk in a sippy cup (drink to thirst)

Tip: Try feeding your child a "rainbow" of solid foods throughout the day so that she gets a variety of nutrition. For example, if you serve something green for lunch, try serving something yellow for a snack, something orange for dinner, etc. To maintain a balanced diet, try feeding your child a fruit, a vegetable, a protein, and a grain throughout the course of the day.

15 MONTHS PLUS: EXPERT LEVEL EATER!
(PLUS COMMON FOOD ISSUES)

At this stage, your child can eat just about anything the rest of the family enjoys, so congrats on getting to this point! And, so long as you've been following the tips and tools we've provided, there should hardly be any cooking or preparing separate foods for your toddler. What a relief!

The main points to remember in this stage are:

- YOUR CHILD MAY SUDDENLY EAT LESS. Your one-time food champ might now eat only a few bites before signaling she's all done. Do not be alarmed! Toddlers are busy little people now, always on the run. It's normal. What's important here is that you stay with the routine of set mealtimes, even if they eat only a few bites each time they sit down.

- LOCATION MATTERS. At your kitchen table, your toddler may refuse every offering of grilled chicken. But at little Peter's birthday party? You may find him in a corner downing it by the plateful! Don't be surprised if this happens—it's a reminder to keep trying different foods, because our babies will continue to surprise us!

- LET THEM HELP. The more interested they can become in the process of making a meal, the more likely they will be to try it. Allow them to spread some hummus on their sandwich bread (perhaps with the back of a spoon, for safety reasons), or allow them to add ingredients to the blender for a smoothie. At the very least, invite them to watch you prepare meals, and talk to them about the ingredients or aroma as you cook.

- HAVE SOME FAVORITES READY IN THE FREEZER. We recommend you find some of your baby's favorite meals from our book that are freezer friendly and have them prepared in your freezer for busy nights. There are plenty of times we are too busy to cook or have an adult night out planned and need something quick to grab for our toddlers—and having healthy portions within arm's reach is much better than fast foods! And it's great peace of mind for us, knowing that "fast" can also equal "nutritious."

- TRY, TRY AGAIN. Food your baby loves today, he may reject tomorrow. The meal he devoured this week, he won't touch next week. This can be a fickle phase, and your toddler definitely has more opinions and is asserting his independence. As difficult as it may be (we know, we've been there!), try to remain calm, patient, and confident in what you're doing. Know that this is just a phase that will pass, and your hard work will pay off in the end! Just be prepared for it and take solace in knowing that it will pass.

- DON'T GIVE UP ON MEATS. It is extremely common at this age for children to become less receptive to meats, so if this sounds familiar, know that you are not alone! There are many possible reasons for their newfound meat aversion, so we recommend you do not give up entirely. Instead, visit our "Helpful Tips" chapter, where we have great information on how to help your child through this "meat fickle" stage.

Look for the following icons on each recipe to determine how it can be served:

PUREE	MASHED	SPOON FEED	SELF FEED	FAMILY FRIENDLY

GRANDMA'S ENGLISH
MUFFIN PIZZAS

AGE 15 months plus
YIELD 12 pizza muffins
FOOD STORAGE refrigerator friendly, freezer friendly
PREP TIME 8 minutes
COOK TIME 12 minutes

This recipe is a family favorite for Ali, inspired by her grandmother. When she re-created the recipe in her kitchen, she was immediately transported to being a little girl in her grandmother's kitchen, helping her make these delicious little pizzas. The bubbly cheese, just the right amount of sauce, and the perfect size pizzas for her little hands equaled a savory, special dinner. It's no surprise that she couldn't wait to make these for her daughter Penelope!

We love these for our book because they are fun for kids, easy to make, and you'll have plenty to freeze for later—including a nice batch of sauce! You won't find any pizza grease here. This recipe yields six "classic style" pizzas and six "white slice" pizzas, but don't hesitate to get creative and add more of your family's favorite toppings!

INGREDIENTS

- 6 whole grain English muffins (1 package), sliced in halves
- ¾ cup tomato sauce (use your favorite store-bought brand, or make your own large batch of sauce; recipe on following page)
- ¾ cup shredded mozzarella cheese
- ¾ cup fresh ricotta cheese
- 5 cherry tomatoes, sliced into thirds
- Drizzle (approximately 1 tablespoon) of extra virgin olive oil

1 Preheat the oven to 375 degrees.

2 Arrange the English muffin halves in a single layer on a baking sheet (you should have 12 pieces).

3 Spoon approximately 1½–2 tablespoons of sauce onto each of 6 English muffins, gently spreading with the spoon to cover. Top each one with approximately 2 tablespoons of shredded mozzarella cheese.

4 Spread 1½–2 tablespoons of ricotta cheese onto each of the remaining 6 English muffins, then top with pieces of sliced tomatoes, and drizzle with olive oil. (At this point, set aside any pizzas you will be freezing for later, store in an airtight freezer bag, and place in the freezer.)

5 Bake the pizzas for approximately 10 minutes or until the cheese starts to bubble.

6 Switch your oven to broil mode, and broil for 1–2 minutes or until the cheese starts to lightly brown. Remove from the oven, allow to cool, then serve. Buon appetito!

BASIC MARINARA SAUCE

Here is Ali's basic marinara sauce, inspired by her mother's and tweaked by Ali over the years. It creates a nice, large batch, which you can freeze into portions for many future dinners of pasta, chicken or eggplant parmesan, and more. We find it to be delicious and simple, with just the right amount of sweetness thanks to the cinnamon. Enjoy!

INGREDIENTS

- ½ cup extra virgin olive oil
- 8 garlic cloves, minced
- 2 (28-ounce) cans crushed tomatoes (preferably organic and in BPA-free cans)
- 1 (28-ounce) can tomato puree (preferably organic and in a BPA-free can)
- ½ yellow onion
- 2 tablespoons Italian seasoning
- 1 tablespoon ground cinnamon
- 2 teaspoons kosher salt
- 2 teaspoons fresh ground black pepper
- 2 tablespoons fresh oregano, minced (can use 1 tablespoon dried oregano as an alternative)
- Handful fresh basil leaves

Tip: Before you begin, be sure to have the cans of tomatoes opened and all of the garlic cloves minced. This will allow you to pour the sauce into the pot as soon as the recipe calls for it, and add the garlic all at once to keep it from burning. Also, the half of the onion will be added to the sauce in one piece, therefore there is no reason to slice, dice, or chop it beforehand.

1 Place a large sauce pot over medium heat. Add the olive oil and heat for 1 minute. Add the garlic to the pot, and stir continuously for 30 seconds to prevent burning. Add the cans of crushed tomatoes and tomato puree. Stir well.

2 Place the ½ of the yellow onion into the pot of sauce. (The onion is there for flavor and will be removed later; do not chop into smaller pieces.) Add the Italian seasoning, cinnamon, salt, and pepper. Stir to combine. Bring the sauce to a low boil, and then reduce the heat to a simmer. Add the fresh oregano and simmer with the cover resting on top of pot, tilted so it is not sealed, for 25–30 minutes, stirring occasionally.

3 Taste the sauce and adjust the flavor to your liking if necessary by adding additional salt/pepper/ herbs/spice to taste. Remove from the heat. Tear the basil leaves into small pieces using your hands, drop into the pot, and stir to combine.

4 Allow the sauce to cool. Using a slotted spoon, remove the large piece of onion. Use the sauce for our English muffin pizzas or over pasta, and freeze the remaining sauce in pint- or quart-size portions.

OKRA WHEELS
WITH TURMERIC

AGE 15 months plus
YIELD approximately 2½–3 cups
FOOD STORAGE refrigerator friendly
PREP TIME 5 minutes
COOK TIME 8 minutes

Okra is a vegetable that often gets overlooked by parents because many adults assume their kid may not care for the texture. This recipe presents warm, subtle Indian flavors of okra that your little one might love as much as ours do! Just make sure you put a full coverage bib on your tot while he's enjoying this, as turmeric can stain!

INGREDIENTS

- 1 tablespoon extra virgin olive oil
- 3 cups sliced okra rounds, approximately ½-inch thick
- ½ teaspoon ground turmeric
- ½ teaspoon ground cumin
- ½ teaspoon ground coriander
- ¼ teaspoon kosher salt
- Juice of ¼ lemon, seeds removed

1 Heat the oil in a medium-size sauté pan over medium heat. Add the okra and cook for about 2 minutes, stirring occasionally. Sprinkle the turmeric, cumin, coriander, and salt over the okra. Mix well. Cook the okra an additional 2–4 minutes or until tender.

2 Promptly remove the okra rounds from the heat before they become too soggy. Add the lemon juice and stir. Serve, cutting the okra into bite-size pieces appropriate for your toddler.

The chemicals in turmeric may decrease inflammation.

JACK AND THE BEAN SALAD

AGE 15 months plus

YIELD approximately 5-6 cups

FOOD STORAGE refrigerator friendly, freezer friendly

PREP TIME 6 minutes

COOK TIME no cook!

This healthy side dish was inspired by a recipe Amy's sister-in-law, Ann, served at Thanksgiving one year. Everyone loved it, including Amy's toddler! The beans were easy for him to pick up and eat with his hands, and the nutrition-packed ingredients were a bonus for the whole family!

INGREDIENTS

- 15 ounces canned black beans
- 15 ounces canned garbanzo beans
- 16 ounces frozen edamame, preferably organic, straight from the freezer
- 16 ounces frozen corn, preferably organic, straight from the freezer
- 2 tablespoons extra virgin olive oil
- 2 tablespoons organic apple cider vinegar with the "mother"
- 1½ tablespoons balsamic vinegar
- ½ teaspoon kosher salt

1 Place the black beans, garbanzo beans, frozen edamame, and frozen corn in a large colander and rinse thoroughly with cool water to remove excess sodium. Drain thoroughly, then transfer the mixture to a large mixing bowl.

2 Add the oil, both vinegars, and salt to the bowl. Mix well and serve!

THE AVOCADO, TOMATO,
HUMMUS SANDWICH

AGE 15 months plus
YIELD 1 sandwich
FOOD STORAGE best if served immediately
PREP TIME approximately 5 minutes
COOK TIME no cook!

This recipe was inspired from Amy's days living in San Francisco. She and her friends would pack these simple ingredients in a brown paper bag and go for a hike in Northern California. Once they reached the top of the mountain, they'd cut the ingredients using a pocket knife, assemble their sandwiches, and have a picnic under a shady tree, savoring the simple ingredients and breathtaking view!

Don't be surprised if your little one typically doesn't care much for avocado or hummus but still enjoys this sandwich—many moms have told us that despite not favoring one of these ingredients, their toddler still enjoyed this one.

"This sandwich is more than just the sum of its parts. The carotenoids in the tomatoes work as antioxidants, helping to neutralize free radicals, which cause cell damage. However, they are not absorbed well if a tomato is eaten alone. The carotenoids are fat soluble and become more bioavailable mixed with the fat from the avocado."—Dr. Elissa Levine, pediatrician.

INGREDIENTS

- ⅛ teaspoon fresh lemon juice
- 1 tablespoon avocado, mashed
- 1 slice whole wheat bread
- 1 tablespoon store-bought hummus
- 1–2 tomato slices, sliced paper thin

1 In a small bowl, add the lemon juice to the mashed avocado. Mix well to prevent browning.

2 Cut the bread down the middle to create two equal halves. Evenly spread the mashed avocado onto one of the halves. Evenly spread hummus onto the other half, then top with tomato slices. Place the bread with the mashed avocado on top to create a sandwich. Be sure to give it a good press so that the halves stick together!

3 Cut the sandwich in half or into bite-sized pieces appropriate for your toddler. Serve! To store the unused portion of avocado for later, sprinkle fresh lemon juice on the flesh, place it in an airtight container, and refrigerate and use within 24 hours.

KRISPY KALE CHIPS

AGE 15 months plus

YIELD 4-6 cups chips

FOOD STORAGE store in an airtight container for up to 3 days

PREP TIME 10 minutes

COOK TIME 10 minutes

Ali had been searching for a way to creatively—and simply—serve her daughter Penelope kale, as it of course is a powerhouse food from a nutritional standpoint. She had a hunch her daughter would like these "chips," but was not prepared for just how easily she'd gobble them up! Between the two of them, they devoured the first batch within minutes!

Kale has protein, fiber, vitamin C, manganese, calcium, and a host of other vitamins and minerals. We paired it with omega-rich flaxseed and beneficial turmeric, turning it into a flavorful, nutritious side dish or snack. These chips are guilt free and supereasy to make, and you're guaranteed to have fun crunching away with your little one! Be sure to offer your tot plenty of milk or water between bites, as the chips can be a bit dry.

INGREDIENTS

- 1 bunch kale leaves, rinsed and ribs removed (approximately 4–6 cups)
- 2 tablespoons extra virgin olive oil
- 1 teaspoon ground flaxseed
- ¼ teaspoon ground turmeric
- ¼ teaspoon kosher salt
- ¼ teaspoon ground black pepper

Flaxseed are an excellent source of omega-3 essential fatty acids and fiber. It is also a known bulking laxative (can help firm-up stool).

Tip: To save time, purchase fresh, prewashed kale leaves from the grocery store.

1 Preheat oven to 425 degrees.

2 Use a paper towel or a salad spinner to completely dry the kale leaves of any water. (This will help them crisp up nicely.) Loosely tear kale leaves into large pieces.

3 In a large mixing bowl, combine the oil, flaxseed, turmeric, salt, and pepper. Stir to combine. Add the kale leaves to the bowl and mix with your hand or a spoon until all the leaves are coated in the seasoning mixture.

4 Line a baking sheet with foil. Spread the kale leaves evenly onto the baking sheet in a single layer (if you have too much kale to keep in a single layer, use another baking sheet, or simply bake in 2 batches). Bake for 7 minutes, gently turn kale leaves over with a spatula or pair of tongs, and bake for an additional 3 minutes on the other side (the leaves will be lightly browned). Allow them to cool, then serve.

CHANA MASALA

AGE 15 months plus
YIELD approximately 4 cups
FOOD STORAGE refrigerator friendly, freezer friendly
PREP TIME 8 minutes
COOK TIME 16 minutes

When Amy needs a delicious dinner on the table in a hurry, and she doesn't have time to hassle with cooking meat, Chana Masala is a family favorite that she often turns to. The whole family thoroughly enjoys it, and it's a nutritious, one-pot meal that's ready in 25 minutes or less! This recipe is mild enough for toddlers and still delicious enough for adults.

Garbanzo beans are a great source of protein and fiber, and they are easy for toddlers to eat! Try serving this over basmati rice or with hot, toasted naan bread.

INGREDIENTS

Cumin is a good source of iron and has infection-fighting properties.

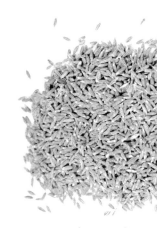

- 2 tablespoons extra virgin olive oil
- ½ yellow onion, diced
- 2 cloves garlic, minced
- 1 teaspoon ginger, minced
- 1 teaspoon cumin seeds
- 2 teaspoons ground coriander
- 1 teaspoon ground turmeric
- 7 ounces canned diced tomatoes, no salt added, preferably organic
- ¾ cup low-sodium vegetable broth, preferably organic
- 2 teaspoons kosher salt
- ½ teaspoon black pepper
- 30 ounces canned garbanzo beans, drained and rinsed
- ½ cup cilantro, minced

1 Heat the oil over medium heat in a large sauté pan. Once the oil is hot, add the onions and sauté for 3–5 minutes or until translucent.

2 Add the garlic, ginger, cumin, coriander, and turmeric. Sauté the mixture for 1–2 minutes, stirring frequently to prevent burning. Add the tomatoes, vegetable broth, salt, pepper, and garbanzo beans. Mix well and bring to a boil.

3 Once boiling, reduce the heat to medium low, and simmer for approximately 5 minutes or until the garbanzo beans are tender. Add the cilantro and mix well. Serve!

Notes: Adults looking for extra spice can add freshly diced jalapeno to the adult portion only.

SLOW-COOKER
CHICKEN TACOS

AGE 15 months plus
YIELD approximately 6 cups
FOOD STORAGE refrigerator friendly, freezer friendly
PREP TIME approximately 5 minutes
COOK TIME 8 hours

Busy parents swear by slow cooking, and we can see why! You drop the ingredients in, set it, and forget it! Toddlers seem to like this dish because the chicken is moist, and the shredded texture of the chicken makes it very palatable for them to eat. This makes a large batch so that you can serve it to the whole family, and you'll still have a whole batch to freeze so that dinner is ready another night!

"Some people love the smell of cilantro, and some people think cilantro smells like soap. There is even a genetic basis for this preference. However, that does not mean that your little one (or even you) cannot grow to enjoy cilantro. Like any other food, repeated exposures makes cilantro more palatable. If traditional chopped cilantro does not appeal to you, try making a cilantro pesto. Crushing the leaves allows natural enzymes to modify the aldehydes that give cilantro its 'soapy' aroma."—Dr. Elissa Levine, pediatrician.

INGREDIENTS

- 1 ¼ pounds boneless, skinless chicken breast, preferably organic
- 15 ounces low-sodium black beans, drained
- 14 ounces frozen corn, preferably organic, straight from freezer
- 16 ounces mild store-bought salsa, preferably organic
- ½ cup water
- 1 teaspoon kosher salt
- ½ teaspoon pepper
- 1 teaspoon ground cumin
- 1 cup fresh cilantro, minced
- Whole wheat tortillas (optional)

1 Add all the ingredients except the cilantro and tortillas (if using) to the slow cooker. (No need to cut the chicken.) Mix the ingredients well.

2 Slow cook on low for approximately 8 hours, undisturbed. The meal is ready when the chicken is fork tender. Shred all of the chicken using a fork and knife. Add the cilantro and mix well.

SERVING OPTIONS

- Create soft tacos: Place the chicken mixture in a whole wheat tortilla. Top with grated cheese and sour cream. Roll the tortilla up to create a soft taco or burrito, then slice it into bite-size circles for your toddler. Adults looking for extra spice can add jalapenos to the adult soft tacos only.
- Create a burrito bowl: place the chicken mixture in a bowl over cooked rice. Top with grated cheese and sour cream. Serve your toddler the burrito bowl with a spoon.

Cilantro can help rid the body of harmful toxins

STRAWBERRY
RICOTTA TOAST

AGE 15 months plus

YIELD 1 serving

FOOD STORAGE best served immediately

PREP TIME approximately 5 minutes

COOK TIME no cook!

This one is so easy, and after Ali made it, she couldn't believe that she never thought to do this before. It was a quick lunch that turned out to be both filling and just the right amount of protein and sweetness. From time to time, try replacing the strawberries with a different kind of fruit, such as cantaloupe, bananas, or fresh peaches!

INGREDIENTS

- 1 piece of whole grain bread
- 2 tablespoons fresh ricotta cheese
- 1 teaspoon honey (preferably local)
- 1 handful of strawberries (preferably organic, rinsed, stems removed, loosely chopped)

1 Toast the bread in a toaster. Mix the ricotta and the honey together in a small bowl. Spread it on a slice of toast. Top with strawberries, and serve. Done!

KIDDIE CRUDITE

AGE 15 months plus
YIELD approximately ¾ cup
FOOD STORAGE refrigerator friendly
PREP TIME approximately 5 minutes
COOK TIME no cook!

When Amy and her husband attended a Super Bowl party, they chose to bring with them the most anti–Super Bowl food there is: fresh vegetables with dipping sauce! She expected this crudite platter to be a hit with the ladies, but was surprised that—even among all the chips and dips—her 2-year-old kept asking for the colorful vegetables!

She'd tried serving raw vegetables on the side of her son's lunch or dinner before, and it was always hit or miss. This event taught her that, just like adults, toddlers eat with their eyes first. Presenting beautiful color blocks of vegetables arranged nicely on a plate can be appealing even to a toddler. The key to making this dish enticing to a kid is in the presentation and in ensuring the vegetables are bite-size right for your toddler. Try serving this as an afternoon snack or for lunch on occasion.

INGREDIENTS

- ¼ cup broccoli florets, chopped into bite-size pieces
- ¼ cup orange or yellow bell pepper, seeds removed, chopped into bite-size pieces
- ¼ cup cucumber, chopped into bite-size pieces
- ¼ cup store-bought hummus or your toddler's favorite dipping sauce (try Greek yogurt, mashed avocado, or salad dressing)

1 Arrange the vegetables in colorful groups on a toddler plate. Place the dipping sauce of choice in the middle. Serve, showing your toddler how to "dip" and eat. Enjoy!

GLOSSARY OF HERBS AND SPICES

BASIL: Basil is believed to be a powerful antioxidant with antibacterial properties. It offers a healthy dose of vitamin A, vitamin K (one teaspoon of basil supplies 85 percent of your daily vitamin K intake), manganese, and magnesium and is a rich source of calcium, potassium, and iron. It's no wonder it's known as "the king of herbs"!

How to preserve fresh basil: Fill a single well (or more if needed) of an ice cube tray about half full with finely chopped herbs, then top off with water and freeze. Once solid, pop out the cubes, place in an airtight freezer bag, and freeze.

CARDAMOM: Cardamom may help ease stomach and intestinal gas and help increase the movement of food through the intestine. It is also a good source of calcium, magnesium, potassium, zinc, and vitamin C and a very good source of iron and manganese. (And, as a bonus for parents, it's a great way to add flavor to your morning coffee!)

CILANTRO: Cilantro is a source of iron, magnesium, and manganese. Cilantro can help rid the body of harmful toxins, such as mercury, aluminum, and lead, and the carotenoids in cilantro provide protection for the liver. Its oils are antimicrobials, which help destroy any stressors to the immune system, and can help ease nausea.

How to preserve fresh cilantro: Fill a single well (or more if needed) of an ice cube tray about half full with finely chopped herbs, then top off with water and freeze. Once solid, pop out the cubes, place in an airtight freezer bag, and freeze.

CINNAMON: Cinnamon is a good source of vitamin K and iron. It can help reduce inflammation, has antioxidant and antiseptic properties, and can help fight bacteria. It is also a known astringent (can help decrease diarrhea), can help reduce gas, and can lower blood sugar.

We love cinnamon because it adds a bit of sweetness to foods without adding the harmful surge of sugar in the bloodstream.

CORIANDER: Coriander may help digestion problems, such as upset stomach and gas. Some breastfeeding women use coriander to increase milk flow.

CLOVE: Clove may be antibacterial and acts as an astringent (can help decrease diarrhea). Clove is believed to be an expectorant (expectorants make it easier to cough up phlegm).

CUMIN: Cumin may relieve bloating and gas, is a good source of iron, and has infection-fighting properties.

DILL: Dill is used to aid digestion problems and intestinal gas. It is also anti-inflammatory.

How to preserve fresh dill: Rinse the dill thoroughly under cold running water, then pat dry with a paper towel. Place on a cookie sheet and freeze for four hours (or overnight), then transfer the frozen sprigs to a freezer bag. To use in the future, pull out the desired amount and use as you would fresh dill (it thaws very quickly).

GARLIC: Garlic can be used to help reduce the risk of cancer and build the immune system, and is known to decrease inflammation. It also acts as an antioxidant, as well as suppresses the growth of bacteria. It is both antifungal and antiviral and enhances the body's natural defense system.

GINGER: Ginger contains chemicals that may reduce nausea and inflammation. It is a known antioxidant, can reduce gas, supports the immune system, enhances the body's natural defense system, increases circulation, aids digestion, and can help kill off harmful bacteria. Ginger nourishes and supports the normal function of the blood vessels.

MINT: The oil in mint is thought to calm the stomach and reduce gas. Mint can also help relax the bronchial muscles, which permits easier breathing. It also contains powerful antioxidants, including vitamins A and C.

How to preserve fresh mint: Fill a single well (or more if needed) of an ice cube tray about half full with finely chopped herbs, then top off with water and freeze. Once solid, pop out the cubes, place in an airtight freezer bag, and freeze.

NUTMEG: Nutmeg is believed to ease diarrhea, nausea, stomach pain, and gas. Nutmeg may also be antibacterial and anti-fungal and is a good source of manganese.

OREGANO: Oregano may help reduce cough and aid in digestion. It is believed to be antibacterial, antiviral, and antifungal.

How to preserve fresh oregano: Fill a single well (or more if needed) of an ice cube tray about half full with finely chopped herbs, then top off with water and freeze. Once solid, pop out the cubes, place in an airtight freezer bag, and freeze.

PARSLEY: Parsley may stimulate the appetite and improve digestion. It provides vitamin A carotenoids, which protect eye health, and vitamin K. It may also help ease constipation and intestinal gas. We love it because it helps to add flavor to dishes without adding sodium.

How to preserve fresh parsley: Fill a single well (or more if needed) of an ice cube tray about half full with finely chopped herbs, then top off with water and freeze. Once solid, pop out the cubes, place in an airtight freezer bag, and freeze.

PEPPER: Pepper may help fight germs and increase the flow of digestive juices in the stomach.

ROSEMARY. Rosemary may help boost the immune system and improve blood circulation. It is also a known astringent (can help decrease diarrhea), can aid in digestion, and supplies polyphenols to help reduce bacteria responsible for bloating.

How to preserve fresh rosemary: Fill a single well (or more if needed) of an ice cube tray about half full with finely chopped herbs, then top off with water and freeze. Once solid, pop out the cubes, place in an airtight freezer bag, and freeze.

SAGE: Sage may help stomach pain, bloating, and gas. It is anti-inflammatory and an astringent (can help decrease diarrhea).

How to preserve fresh sage: Fill a single well (or more if needed) of an ice cube tray about half full with finely chopped herbs, then top off with water and freeze. Once solid, pop out the cubes, place in an airtight freezer bag, and freeze.

THYME: Thyme contains chemicals that may help bacterial and fungal infections and has antioxidant properties. It may also relax the bronchial muscles, which permits easier breathing and eases coughing. It also contains iron and vitamin C.

How to preserve fresh thyme: Fill a single well (or more if needed) of an ice cube tray about half full with finely chopped herbs, then top off with water and freeze. Once solid, pop out the cubes, place in an airtight freezer bag, and freeze.

TURMERIC. The chemicals in turmeric may decrease inflammation. It is an antioxidant, supports liver function and protects liver cells from damage, and may ease diarrhea and intestinal gas.

The following sources were referenced for this Glossary: Cleveland Clinic (http://health.clevelandclinic.org/), The World's Healthiest Foods (http://whfoods.com), USDA National Nutrient Database (http://ndb.nal.usda.gov/ndb/foods), WebMD (http://www.webmd.com/), and the reference book *Herbal Medicine from the Heart of the Earth*.

MEALS READY IN ABOUT
30 MINUTES OR LESS

Whether you are a working parent or a stay-at-home parent and whether you have one child or five, every parent is pressed for time, and cooking can be challenging. The following recipes can be prepared and on the table in about 30 minutes or less—perfect for busy weeknights or times when you need to feed hungry mouths in a hurry!

6 MONTHS PLUS

- *Birthday Suit Bananas*
- *Only Oats*
- *Velvety Prunes*
- *Clean Carrots*
- *Plain Peas*
- *Bare Pear*
- *Creamy Avocado*
- *Cocoa Avocado Smoothie for Parent*

8 MONTHS PLUS

- *Roasted Salmon with Pear and Lime*
- *Fruity Fusion*
- *Blueberries with Spinach*
- *Bananas with Cinnamon*
- *Please more Peas*
- *Sow Your Oats?*
- *Baby Green Machine*
- *Cauliflower Apple Steamer*

10 MONTHS PLUS

- *Kale with Garlic and Ginger*
- *Zucchini and Squash Bites with Rosemary*
- *Strawberry Banana Greek Yogurt*
- *Mediterranean Couscous with Feta, Lemon, and Parsley*
- *Coconut Curry Goan Fish*
- *Baby Gazpacho*

12 MONTHS PLUS

- *Cool Cucumber Sandwich Bites*
- *Five O'Clock Pasta*
- *Poached Eggs*
- *Basil and Kale Frittata*
- *Baby Caprese Salad*
- *Baby Beef and Greens*
- *Parsi Rava: An Indian Spin on Cream of Wheat*
- *Scarborough Fair Grilled Cheese*
- *Turkey Cutlets*
- *Spinach and Goat Cheese Mini Muffins*
- *The Almond Butter Banana Boat*

15 MONTHS PLUS

- *Grandma's English Muffin Pizzas*
- *Okra Wheels with Turmeric*
- *Jack and the Bean Salad*
- *The Avocado, Tomato, Hummus Sandwich*
- *Krispy Kale Chips*
- *Chana Masala*
- *Strawberry Ricotta Toast*
- *Kiddie Crudite*

HEALTHY SNACK IDEAS FOR 12 MONTHS AND 15 MONTHS PLUS (AT HOME AND ON THE GO)

HEALTHY SNACK OPTIONS FOR 12-MONTH-OLD

EAT AT HOME:

- *Baby Caprese Salad*
- *The Almond Butter Banana Boat*
- Diced Fruit (mango, kiwi, cantaloupe, pineapple, avocado, etc.)
- Fresh, organic berries (raspberries, blackberries, strawberries, etc.)
- Whole wheat bread with organic almond or peanut butter
- Organic plain yogurt
- Cottage cheese

TAKE TO GO:

- *Spinach and Goat Cheese Mini Muffins*
- Banana
- Diced apple or grapes
- Diced cheese (cheddar, mozzarella, etc.)
- Store-bought, organic applesauce

HEALTHY SNACK OPTIONS FOR 15-MONTH-OLD

EAT AT HOME:

- *Baby Caprese Salad*
- *The Almond Butter Banana Boat*
- *Strawberry Ricotta Toast*
- *Kiddie Crudite*
- Diced fruit (mango, kiwi, cantaloupe, pineapple, avocado, etc.)
- Fresh, organic berries (raspberries, blackberries, strawberries, etc.)
- Whole wheat bread with organic almond or peanut butter
- Organic plain yogurt
- Cottage cheese

TAKE TO GO:

- *Spinach and Goat Cheese Mini Muffins*
- *Krispy Kale Chips*
- Dried fruit (diced apricot, prunes, dates, cranberries, raisins, etc.)
- Banana
- Diced apple or grapes
- Diced cheese (cheddar, mozzarella, etc.)
- Whole wheat crackers
- Diced vegetables (bell pepper, cucumber, etc.)
- Fresh fruit or vegetable smoothie in a sippy cup

FREQUENTLY ASKED QUESTIONS
AND HELPFUL INFORMATION

HOW CAN I TELL IF MY BABY IS READY TO START SOLIDS?

Before we begin feeding solids to our baby, first we need to be sure our baby is indeed ready. This usually happens by 6 months of age, and for some babies as early as 4 or 5 months!

While it is best to consult your child's pediatrician as to when your baby is ready, if your baby is showing most, if not all, of the following signs, it may be time to start feeding him solids:

- Baby can sit up without having to be supported.
- Baby seems interested and eager to participate in mealtimes.
- Baby's appetite is consistently growing (not to be confused with a growth spurt that often occurs between 3 and 4 months).
- Baby has doubled his birth weight.
- Baby does not push food out of his mouth with his tongue (the "extrusion reflex").

Please note: it is when most, if not all, of the above are met that your baby should be ready to begin eating solid foods. Again, check with your baby's pediatrician before you begin.

WHAT ARE THE BENEFITS OF USING HERBS AND SPICES IN MY BABY'S FOOD, AND HOW CAN I DO SO SAFELY?

There are many benefits to adding herbs and spices to your homemade baby food! You're introducing your child to new and interesting flavors at an early age, which can help promote well-rounded eating habits right from the start. You're making foods instantly more palatable without reaching for the salt. Many of them have known benefits. The list goes on and on! We've taken much care and research to show you just how you can do it within each of our recipes.

Dee Harris, a registered, licensed, and certified dietitian, nutritionist, and diabetes educator whom we interviewed for our book, agreed that herbs and spices are safe and can be beneficial to babies—and added that they can be detoxifying as well. She recommends that we treat them the same as we treat new foods, introducing them one at a time and using the *"four-day wait rule"* before trying another. (For more information on all of the herbs and spices we use in our recipes, see our "Glossary of Herbs and Spices.")

Although they are safe, you should understand that a little bit goes a long way and always be respectful to your baby's sensitive palate. Dr. Maya Shetreat-Klein, integrative pediatric neurologist and herbalist, advised us that most spices are fine in moderation, and it's best to be sure we don't get too aggressive. You will find that each of our recipes highlights the benefit of the herb or spice used and includes appropriate measurements.

AT WHAT AGE CAN MY BABY HAVE SALT?

There is often much concern over just how much salt is OK for a baby: Should a baby be sodium free for the first year? Is a little bit safe? And just how much is "a little bit"?

We had the same concerns when it was time to feed our little ones, which is why we consulted several doctors and specialists for their input while creating this book.

We prefer not to add any salt prior to 12 months of age, as the sodium requirements for this age group are remarkably low—only 400 milligrams of sodium per day," advises Dr. Elissa Levine, pediatrician. *"Until 6 months of age, breast milk or formula provides all the sodium babies need. Also, we are trying to prime babies' palates not to prefer salty foods. Children who like salt become adults who like salt. Give your child a gift that will last a lifetime by minimizing added salt in his or her diet.*

And, when discussing salt after a baby's first year, Dr. Levine adds: *"While I love using herbs and spices to season foods, using a modest amount of salt is acceptable at this stage. You should be quite comfortable using small amounts in some of your homemade baby food, especially if you are mostly avoiding processed foods."*

So there you have it: salt in moderation is OK after one year, just don't go reaching for it to add to every meal—mainly because we want to prime babies' palates for healthy sodium consumption as they grow. All of the recipes in this book that call for salt have been doctor approved for their sodium levels.

Aside from the amount of salt you are adding to a baby's food (as well as the family's food), we discovered that there is a great deal of importance in the *type* of salt being used. As it turns out, a key ingredient—iodine—is extremely important in a child's diet, and not all salts contain iodine.

I have seen some children get goiters here in the United States of America when iodized salt was completely avoided and the families did not eat out much, and/or the child was in a growth spurt," explains JuliSu DiMucci-Ward, registered dietitian, certified diabetes educator, and a specialist in pediatric nutrition. *"When salt is used after 12 months, I recommend iodized in most cases because the soil in the United States is poor in iodine. Not many individuals get enough iodine from shellfish, fish, or seaweed here in the United States.*

CAN I SERVE MY BABY LEFTOVERS?

In the early days of feeding our babies, we often wondered: Is it OK for us to feed them the same food a couple of days in a row? After all, we are preparing the meals ourselves, and many of the recipes produce large quantities. We looked to a few registered dieticians for answers, and it turns out, the answer is yes, it is OK.

"There is nothing wrong with feeding food several days in a row," explains Registered Dietitian Stacey Vanderwel. *"Focus more on if they are getting a variety on a daily, even weekly basis (i.e., don't give them the same meal for breakfast, lunch, and dinner)."*

Looking at the bigger picture in terms of daily food intake as well as weekly will help you avoid what JuliSu DiMucci-Ward, registered dietitian and pediatric specialist in nutrition, calls *"taste fatigue."* This is when a baby's taste buds grow tired of a favorite food, causing her to refuse it.

"Children (and adults) often have food 'jags' and keep repeating the same food choice again and again. If foods are not rotated, children will eventually tire of a food and then reject it—sometimes for the longest of times."

To avoid this, she encourages rotating the foods as much as possible.

FREQUENTLY ASKED QUESTIONS

WHEN IS IT MOST IMPORTANT TO BUY ORGANIC PRODUCE?

We note throughout the book instances where we recommend purchasing food that is grown organically versus conventionally if possible. This is important for certain foods; for example, blueberries (or many berries in particular) may contain high levels of pesticide residue, which is why we recommend purchasing organic if possible.

If purchasing organic food is not a viable option due to price or availability, you can purchase conventionally grown fruits or vegetables, soak them in a diluted vinegar bath for a few minutes, and then thoroughly rinse them off before consuming. This will remove some of the pesticides found in the outer part of the fruit/vegetable that you cannot scrub or peel.

SHOULD I PEEL THE FRUITS AND VEGETABLES I SERVE TO MY BABY?

When it comes to what we serve our babies, since we choose to purchase organic, we keep the peels intact for most fruits and vegetables. We feel this is important because there are nutrients contained in the peel. Naturopathic Doctor Stephanie Mottola confirms our research: *"When buying organic produce, washing the skins should suffice. In fact, there are often many nutrients concentrated in the skin of fruits and veggies. If a baby is in generally good health, raw, pureed fruits will most likely be fine when starting solid foods."*

WHICH FOODS ARE "SUPERFOODS"?

When we asked about *"superfoods,"* every doctor and specialist we interviewed agreed: they can often be spotted simply by paying attention to their color. In other words, the foods that are most *colorful in their natural form* tend to all be superfoods. Therefore, an easy way to be sure we are including a variety of superfoods in our babies' diets is to provide a diverse array of colors.

We can refer to the rainbow, in this instance, but below are some examples:
- RED: beets, pomegranate, raspberries, tomatoes, strawberries
- ORANGE: carrots, sweet potatoes, cantaloupe, pumpkin, mango, orange
- YELLOW: lemon, sweet yellow pepper, ginger, cauliflower, garlic
- GREEN: kale, spinach, kiwi, broccoli, avocado, cucumber
- BLUE: blueberries, blackberries
- PURPLE: figs, prunes, eggplant, purple potatoes

Registered Dietitian JuliSu DiMucci-Ward adds one caveat: *"Excessive orange or yellow veggies may turn the baby's skin an orange hue, because we store beta-carotene in our tissues. It is harmless but often causes parents to worry."*

You'll be happy to know that our recipes are made up of many superfoods!

WHAT TYPES OF OILS ARE BEST TO USE WHEN COOKING FOR MY BABY?

Throughout our recipes, we cook mainly with olive oil or butter, simply because we have found these to be the most healthful, readily available, and versatile ingredients. For butter, we recommend grass fed and organic, and for olive oil, we recommend extra virgin, organic, and cold pressed.

Other healthy oils you can use in moderation, or substitute in some cases, are ghee, coconut oil, and avocado oil.

IS DAIRY SAFE FOR MY BABY BEFORE HER FIRST BIRTHDAY? WHAT ABOUT YOGURT AND CHEESE?

While pediatricians recommend waiting until a baby's first birthday to introduce cow's milk, is it safe to introduce cheese or yogurt any sooner? The answer is yes, in most cases.

"Cheese is a fabulous, nutritionally dense food for your child. You can certainly introduce cultured dairy products such as cheese and yogurt well before a baby's first birthday. Most babies' tummies are not yet ready to have cow's milk be their primary fluid until they are 1 year of age, but cheese and yogurt are generally safe," explains Dr. Levine.

There are, however, instances where dairy may not be the best choice for your baby, and since every child is different, it's always best to see how yours will react. Dr. Mottola explains: *"Consumption of processed cow dairy (pasteurized and homogenized) can contribute to recurring and chronic health problems, especially of the upper respiratory tract (ear infections, allergies, congestion, and asthma), gut, and immune system. Ghee or pasture-raised butter is generally an exception."*

Dr. Shetreat-Klein speaks to this topic as well. *"Avoid cheese with mold, such as blue cheese."* She also recommends trying cheese made from goat's milk or sheep's milk, both of which are generally better tolerated and easier on the stomach than cow's milk. Registered Dietician Dee Harris agrees that goat's cheese and sheep's cheese are generally more nutritious and less processed than cheese made from cow's milk, and she adds that organic cheeses are preferable.

Lastly, dairy may cause inflammation in some cases. Dr. Levine states, *"Milk proteins can cause inflammation in some people. This inflammation may be seen as a runny nose in some children, irritability in others, or can exacerbate underlying illnesses or discomfort...Like with anything else, some children are more sensitive to the pro-inflammatory effects of dairy, and some children are not affected at all. It makes sense to limit dairy, especially milk, when your child is teething if your child is sensitive to the pro-inflammatory effects of dairy. (If it is your child's favorite drink and soothes her rather than making her more mucousy and irritated, then by all means, give it to her.)"*

WHAT ARE THE BENEFITS OF FOODS MADE WITH WHOLE WHEAT AND WHOLE GRAIN?

We believe in the power of whole wheat and whole grains. There are many healthy whole grains you may try, such as farro and bulgur.

We also wondered: What is the difference between whole wheat/whole grain products and white flour products? Are there real benefits of opting for whole wheat/whole grain? We consulted Dr. Levine:

"Whole wheat products are made from the entire wheat kernel, including the healthy fats of the wheat germ and B vitamins and insoluble fiber of the bran. White flour is made from just the carbohydrate-rich endosperm portion of the kernel and is stripped of the bran and germ. If you can't adjust to the taste of whole wheat pasta, try a chickpea-flour-based pasta or a lentil or black bean pasta instead!"

In other words, choosing whole wheat and whole grain over white products can offer us healthy fats and vitamins.

FREQUENTLY ASKED QUESTIONS

WHAT IS BPA , AND SHOULD I AVOID IT?

BPA stands for bisphenol A and is often found in the liners of food cans. BPA is known to affect the brain and behavior of animals, and for this reason, we recommend purchasing products that say *"BPA free"* on the label whenever possible. We especially recommend this when purchasing tomato products. The high acidity of tomatoes allows BPA from the liner to leech into the food. It's always better to purchase tomato products in glass jars or cans that are BPA free whenever possible. Infants and children metabolize BPA more slowly, and for this reason, the effects of exposure can be more pronounced.

WHEN IS IT OK TO INTRODUCE NUTS TO MY BABY'S DIET?

A nut allergy is a serious subject and one that we as parents and caregivers should always consider.

Dr. Levine states: *"Guidelines for introducing nuts into your child's diet seem to be continually in flux. We do know that more and more children are allergic to foods than ever before. However, avoiding nuts until children are older does not seem to prevent nut allergies. In fact, children in Israel, who are commonly introduced to peanut flour between 8 and 14 months of age, have particularly low incidence of nut allergies."*

The information regarding allergies is, as Dr. Levine states, *"in flux."* Because of this, we recommend you consult your child's pediatrician before serving any foods that are known allergens to get the most up-to-date information and guidelines.

WHAT SHOULD I LOOK FOR WHEN PURCHASING MEATS?

We do not have a set type of diet we follow; rather, we focus a great deal on quality of ingredients. For this reason, we opt for grass-fed, organic meats, and we like to get them from local suppliers and local farmers' markets whenever possible.

A word on grass-fed beef from Dr. Levine: *"If you can stand the sticker shock, grass-fed beef does have advantages over grain-fed beef. Grass-fed beef is generally leaner with fewer calories per serving. The fats are healthier with a higher proportion of omega-3s. However, because it has less fat, grass-fed beef needs to be cooked carefully and often requires less time in the oven than grain-fed beef. Also, grass-fed beef can have a darker color, as it has more beta carotene."*

WHAT SHOULD I LOOK FOR WHEN PURCHASING FISH?

We believe fish can be a great addition to a baby's diet. Certain fish provide wonderful nutrients, such as omega-3 and DHA, to support your little one's growing brain and bones.

When selecting the proper fish to feed to your child, Registered Dietitian Dee Harris advises: *"Stay away from fish that is known to be high in mercury (such as tuna and swordfish), as well as farm-raised fish."* We second this advice and recommend looking for *"wild-caught"* fish at your local fish market or grocery.

Texture is very important too. If your child rejects a food, it is often due to its *texture*, not taste. This can be very relevant when it comes to fish. We recommend beginning with a nice puree, such as our *Roasted Salmon with Pear and Lime* recipe, and sticking with fish that is light, soft, and flaky as the baby gets older.

FEEDING SCHEDULES AND PORTION SIZES: AT WHAT TIMES SHOULD I FEED MY BABY, AND HOW MUCH SHOULD SHE BE EATING?

Every child is different, so there are no hard and fast rules to follow. We do, however, have some general guidelines for you to begin with for each age group, which we've crafted for your convenience. You'll find these pediatrician-approved "*Sample Food Schedules*," which suggest portion sizes, feeding times, and meals to serve, at the beginning of each chapter of recipes. Remember that these are just examples and that you should use your intuition, read your baby's cues, and consult your baby's pediatrician with questions.

ARE CERTAIN VITAMINS PARTICULARLY IMPORTANT?

While consulting the clinical experts for our book, we discovered just how important vitamins and nutrients are for our little ones – especially vitamins A and C.

According to Dr. Mottola: "*Vitamins A and C are integral to healthy immune system function. Vitamin A helps support healthy vision, especially night vision, healthy growth and bone development, healthy skin and mucus membrane integrity and function, and has anti-cancer properties. Vitamin C is important for connective tissue integrity, helps increase the absorption of iron, is involved in steroid hormone (sex hormone) synthesis, detoxification reactions, cancer prevention, degradation of cholesterol, the activation of certain vitamins into their active forms, has anti-histamine effects, and is one of the body's most potent antioxidants.*"

For the reasons above, we incorporated vitamins A and C into many of our recipes. As a general rule, foods that are orange and yellow (in their natural state) tend to be high in beta-carotene, which is converted to vitamin A in the body.

CAN HERBS, SPICES, OR OTHER NATURAL INGREDIENTS HELP WITH COMMON AILMENTS?

We were excited to learn from the doctors we've consulted that yes, foods such as herbs and spices and other natural ingredients in moderate amounts can potentially help with common ailments. We've listed some examples below. (As always, it is best to consult your child's pediatrician or naturopath regarding any illness your child may have or methods of treatment you may use.)

- GAS/UPSET STOMACH: peppermint essential oil on baby's stomach (Registered Dietitian Dee Harris); fennel seed, chamomile (Dr. Shetreat-Klein)
- COLIC: probiotic supplement (Registered Dietitian Dee Harris)
- EAR INFECTIONS: eliminate dairy (Registered Dietitian Dee Harris)
- COLDS: deficient in micronutrients, vitamin C through food, diet in colorful foods (Registered Dietitian Dee Harris)
- IMMUNITY BOOSTING: probiotics, yogurt, fermented veggies such as sauerkraut, kim chi (Registered Dietitian Dee Harris); garlic, bone broths (Dr. Shetreat-Klein)

Lastly, it's helpful to know that a diet abundant in "*superfoods*" can help with a child's overall health and prevent ailments and/or lessen their severity. Dr. Mottola adds: "*Colorful fruits and vegetables are high in antioxidants. Antioxidants protect our cells and every tissue in our body from damage and can help relieve symptoms of allergies and congestion.*"

FREQUENTLY ASKED QUESTIONS

WHICH FOODS ARE KNOWN ALLERGENS, AND SHOULD I AVOID THEM ENTIRELY?

Allergies should be taken very seriously, especially when it comes to our babies. As parents, we should be aware of ingredients that are high on the allergen scale and the signs and symptoms to look for in our children. Foods that tend to be high on the allergen list are:

- Fish
- Eggs
- Dairy
- Nuts
- Soy

We use these ingredients in our recipes in moderation and introduce them at age-appropriate times. As with any foods, the general rule when trying something new is to introduce only one new food at a time and to wait four days in between. This allows enough time for your baby to process the food and show signs of an allergy if one exists.

The above list is just an example. Please note that there are many foods which could produce an allergic reaction. If you have any questions about your child's specific allergies, contact your child's pediatrician.

WHAT'S ONE THING I SHOULD REMEMBER WHEN FEEDING MY BABY?

Lastly, one of the most common themes throughout our book, and what we found while feeding our own children, is to remember to try, try again. Babies and toddlers are unpredictable little creatures: one day they love something, the next day they want nothing to do with it. They launch their fish dinner off of their high chairs tonight, yet tomorrow they'll eat an entire tray of fish at the buffet. Maybe you've given up on green beans because they rejected them multiple times early on, but as a toddler, they may love them. There's no way to tell! For these reasons, we recommend that you always keep an open mind and "try, again and again." Remember that texture, food preparation, environment, and many other factors come into play. Use this chapter and our "Helpful Tips" chapter to guide you along the way.

Remember that your hard work and perseverance will pay off in the end, helping to make your child the best little eater he can be!

HELPFUL TIPS

HELPFUL HINTS ON STARTING SOLID FOODS

BEGIN SLOWLY. Start with single-ingredient purees, like the ones you will find in our 6 Months Plus chapter. We designed our book so that the earliest recipes are single ingredients—the "building blocks" for the recipes we introduce as your baby grows.

WATCH FOR ALLERGIES. The recipes in this book, in the early stages, contain foods that are low on the allergen scale. To be sure there is no allergic reaction, we suggest waiting four days before introducing another new food, herb, or spice to your child. This will allow enough time to see if a particular food is causing a reaction and will eliminate any confusion as to what could be the cause.

A LITTLE GOES A LONG WAY. At the early stages of feeding your baby, a single teaspoon or tablespoon can equal an entire meal for little tummies! Don't worry much about quantity right now. Introducing foods is also about getting your baby used to many other things: eating real food, acclimating to the concept of using a spoon, chewing and swallowing, new textures, new smells, etc.

PAY ATTENTION TO YOUR BABY'S CUES. Some babies are fed their first taste of food and go hog wild, and you'll have to do all you can to keep them from eating the spoon! Others start out more cautious and might need a little coaxing from Mom or Dad. Remember not to push. Let your baby lead the way, and if you see him turn away or become frustrated, take a break. Also, while it may sound silly, it helps if you smile and keep a positive voice, no matter what kind of funny faces they make while eating the food! Babies tend to mimic their caregivers and will look to you to set the tone. The more positive you keep things, the greater experience you will have together!

PAY ATTENTION TO COLOR (REMEMBER 'THE RAINBOW'). We focus a great deal on natural, whole foods to feed your baby. With this in mind, a simple way to be sure your child is receiving a good balance of adequate nutrition is to pay attention to the colors on your baby's plate. Over the course of a week, aim to have a representative from each color of the rainbow: think red (beets), orange (carrots, sweet potatoes), yellow (turmeric), green (spinach, peas, kale), blue (blueberries), and purple (prunes). These are just examples, but keep your eye out for a balance of foods and spices that present these vibrant colors, and use our recipes to guide you along the way.

RETRY FOODS OVER AND OVER. A big mistake parents can make is to assume that their baby doesn't like a particular food after a few attempts at serving it. On average, a baby needs to try a food between 10 and 20 times to be given a chance to accept a new flavor, and some will say it takes even more than that! Take a break if a food is simply not well received. Just be sure you stay open to trying it again at a later date, possibly prepared a different way.

TEXTURE IS KEY. Texture is a factor most babies are particular about. If a food in its solid form isn't working, or if a puree is very thick, try blending and re-serving, adding liquid (water, breast milk, or formula) if needed. If they turn away from a puree (and are at a stage where they are eating more solid, textured foods), offer it cut up into tiny bite-size pieces. They also may be more likely to try it once they touch it and explore it, which is a big part of the eating process for babies.

THIN OUT A PUREE IF NEEDED. Simply add breast milk, formula, or water until you reach the desired consistency. It's always best to begin with a small amount of liquid and add more as needed.

LET 'EM GET MESSY. We admit it: this one isn't easy! Watching your baby take the food you've prepped and smear it all over his high chair, face, and hands is not fun when you have to clean up the mess! But there is a great deal of learning going on within that mess, we can assure you, and allowing baby to explore food in this way could help him become more receptive to it. So strip him down to his diaper, and allow him to explore!

DON'T BE AFRAID TO TRY NEW THINGS! The goal of our book is to encourage you to open your baby's palate to a broad spectrum of foods, flavors, textures, and colors. Offering a wide variety early on gives your child a better chance of being accepting of new foods as she grows. Allow her to become the adventurous little eater you would love for her to be! We provide you with many tools inside the beautiful pages of this book.

BE SAFE. Always remember to serve appropriate-size pieces to your baby. When you move on from purees and your little one is beginning to self-feed, don't leave him unattended, and always be aware of potential choking hazards, such as pieces that are too large, any bones or seeds, etc.

TIPS ON FOOD STORAGE

The nice thing about storing baby food is that you do not need a gazillion little plastic containers, and there are many ways to do it! One way is to use ice cube trays. Simply fill an ice cube tray with leftover puree, and once the puree has frozen (usually 24–48 hours), pop out each portion as you would do with ice cubes, and transfer the puree cubes to a resealable plastic freezer bag. You are now free to use the same ice cube tray for the next batch. You can do this over and over again, until you've frozen all of your leftovers. You may also purchase one set of two-and-a-half-ounce airtight containers and one set of four-ounce airtight containers, and use them over and over again for food storage.

ALWAYS LABEL THE BAGS. You might think you'll remember what's in each bag, but we never do! Better to label it by writing the date and the type of food/puree directly on the bag using a marker. You can use a label maker as an alternative (we keep ours in the kitchen drawer for easy access).

THAW FROZEN FOOD SAFELY. You can store baby food in the freezer for up to three months. The best way to thaw it is to leave it in the refrigerator overnight. If you choose to reheat/defrost food in the microwave, do so in in small time increments, and stir frequently while cooling to avoid any pockets of heat.

You may also safely make purees and other foods using frozen vegetables, then refreeze them for up to three months.

HOW TO MAKE FAMILY MEALS A PRIORITY

Ali grew up in a big Italian family where family meals were a regular occurrence. When it came to starting her own family, she just assumed they'd approach meals with the same mentality. Of course they would all eat together!

That was until she had a toddler who ate dinner at five thirty in the afternoon. Many times, her husband Greg doesn't even make it home from work by the time their daughter Penelope is ready for dinner, making even the *idea* of family meals impossible.

We imagine the older our children get, the easier it will be to sync up our dinner schedules, but in the meantime, we've found some helpful tips that allow us to squeeze in a few family meals together per week—even with our "early bird special" little humans. Turns out there are many benefits to eating together as a family at least a few times per week, so the sooner we can start, the better!

It helps to make family meals a priority. We feel it's important to maintain a family approach to eating from the get-go, and we wrote this book to help you do just that. "*Make eating an important part of the day, and be consistent*," explains Registered Dietitian Stacey Vanderwel.

First, let's look at the benefits of family meals, taken from an article referenced in the USDA National Agricultural Library website (it is impressive!):

> Children from families who eat together on a regular basis are more likely to have family support, positive peer influences, and positive adult role models (Fulkerson, Neumark-Sztainer and Story 2006). Family meals provide an environment that encourages communication between the child and caregiver. Building strong family relationships and ties among family members allows children to trust and depend on their caregivers for support. Researchers have shown that family connectedness is associated with a lower chance of engaging in high-risk behaviors such as substance use and violence, and fewer psycho-logical problems, including emotional distress in children. (Eisenberg, Olson, Neumark-Sztainer, Story, and Bearinger 2004; Fulkerson et al. 2006).

And then there's this:

> Researchers also found that the frequency of family dinner increases characteristics such as having a positive view of one's future, being motivated and engaged in school, being committed to learning, and having positive values and positive identity. (Fulkerson et al. 2006)...Eating family meals is associated with improvement in the nutritional quality of the diet, as well as improvements in children's overall well-being.

Positivity, by the bowlful. Here's how we can help serve it up to our family!

1. KEEP IT SIMPLE. It's helpful to remember that this isn't a formal event; it's dinner in your home. Let's make it fun! Choose simple, colorful foods, and make sure to include at least one thing you know your baby will love. Better yet—plan ahead so you can serve leftovers, and you won't have to prep anything at all before you sit everyone down together! Our *Turkey Cutlets* are a great option to make ahead and freeze, so they're ready when you are.

2. START OFF SLOW. If you are currently lacking in the family meal department (*raises hand with you*), don't bite off more than you can chew. Start with a goal of one family meal per week together, and then, when it feels right, try for two, and increase as you see fit. The less pressure you put on yourself, the better your chances are of success. We find that if you or your partner (or both) follow a traditional work schedule of a Monday–Friday grind, the best day to start incorporating a family meal is on Sunday. And you don't have to limit it to dinner, either; even a simple lunch or breakfast with your little one counts! So long as you eat together.

3. LET YOUR BABY BE INVOLVED–OR AT LEAST WATCH. While Penelope is still too small to help me start chop-ping away, what she can do is watch. I'll often sit her in her high chair and slide it over to where I am preparing din-ner. When you do this, talk to your baby as you chop, and tell her what you're doing. If appropriate, after you chop a slice of food such as a piece of tomato, give it to your toddler so she can explore it! Another option is to give your baby a shatterproof bowl and spoon, and let her play with that as you chop and prep.

4. HAVE YOUR CHILD HELP YOU. It's also never too early to teach children how to help. Clear out a low drawer in the kitchen and make it just for them: plates, bibs, spoons, sippy cups. When it's time for dinner, direct your child to the drawer and ask him to help you by getting what is needed for his dinner time. Every morning, I ask Penelope to "go get mama a bib, and we'll have breakfast!" and she is so proud to run over to her little cabinet, fish out a bib, and hand it to me. It's the little things!

5. BE PATIENT, AND TRUST YOURSELF AS A PARENT. According to the Ellyn Satter Institute: "*What works is good parenting with feeding: have regular family meals, serve the child the same food as the rest of the family, trust the child to eventually learn to eat those foods, maybe just not right now. Within a structured feeding environment, the child will do his jobs: eat as much as he needs and learn to eat the foods that parents enjoy. It takes time and patience, but, in the meantime, parents can enjoy family mealtime.*" (See more at: http://ellynsatterinstitute.org/fmf/fmf72.php#sthash.pgi0fauV.dpuf)

Registered Dietitian JuliSu DiMucci-Ward adds a few more ideas for getting the most out of family meals:

1. Have soft instrumental music playing in the background and no visual distractions (TV, etc.)
2. For families with older children: Go around the table and have everyone say one nice/good thing about a particular family member. In our home we have a special plate that rotates nightly, so, over the course of the week, we all get it at least once. Whoever has the plate is the topic person for the night!
3. Make eating fun! Always have one food on the table that everyone finds acceptable, and have one night a week for each individual family member to choose the menu; that way everyone has his or her favorite respected.

TOUBLESHOOTING PICKY EATING

"Picky eating" is a common issue among babies and toddlers. It is important to realize that phases of picky eating are almost a certainty, but there are strategies to minimize it, making it more of a phase that children go in and out of versus something more permanent.

Since every child is different (so different!), we consulted Registered Dietitian Lindsey McKeon to provide us with her favorite tips and tricks to minimize picky eating as much as possible. Here is what she recommends:

1. BE PATIENT WITH NEW FOODS. Young children must touch, smell, and explore new foods. In order for your child to feel comfortable eating something, the child has to become familiar with the food.
2. ENCOURAGE YOUR CHILD TO EXPLORE THE FOOD. Let her squeeze it between her fingers and play with it (let go of wanting to clean her up so quickly, it really helps her learn).
3. OFFER SMALL AMOUNTS WHEN INTRODUCING A NEW FOOD. You do not want the child to feel overwhelmed.
4. TRY, TRY AGAIN! Repeat exposure to a new food. Some research has even stated that a child must be presented with a new food 20 times before showing any interest to taste a food.
5. LEAD BY EXAMPLE. Let your child see what you are eating, and let him see you enjoying the food. This is actually a better tip then telling your child, "Eat your (fill in the blank) so you'll get strong!"
6. GET KIDS INVOVLED. If they are old enough, let them help you measure out the ingredients or stir the mixture. Plant a garden, let them see how food grows, water the plants with them, and pick the herbs, fruit, or vegetables that have grown. Take them to the grocery store and let them help you pick out foods.
7. CUT FOODS INTO COOL SHAPES. You can use molds or cookie cutters when trying new foods. Also, there are numerous cool, fun, interactive plates and silverware.
8. DON'T BE A SHORT-ORDER COOK. Many kids will hold out because they know you will eventually give in and prepare the food they want.
9. RESPECT TINY TUMMIES. Offer a nibble plate of each food—do not force-feed.
10. MINIMIZE DISTRACTIONS. Sit down to eat, and have conversation or play soft music. Turning out the lights or dimming the lights can provide a calm environment. We are too anxious that our children will starve, so this can be a helpful reminder for parents to remember to remain calm.
11. OFFER WATER IN BETWEEN MEALS SO THE CHILD DOESN'T FILL UP ON LIQUIDS DURING THE MEAL.

We also love this tip: try serving smaller quantities. In the words of Dr. Levine: *"Be careful about putting too many bite-size sandwich cubes on your little one's food tray. Some children 'overstuff' their mouths, and compacted bread can become a choking hazard if they put handfuls in their mouths. Make sure they swallow before taking the next piece and do not just 'store' the pieces in their little chipmunk cheeks!"*

WAYS TO DISTRACT AND ENTERTAIN YOUR CHILD WHILE YOU COOK

1. Pretend to cook—have a play kitchen set up near the real kitchen.
2. Have a dedicated shelf or cabinet the child may play in and drag toys out of.
3. Have a special, dedicated toy that can only be played with while it's time to cook.
4. Set her in the high chair (depending on age) with magnets, Play-Doh, or stickers with paper.
5. Offer her a cooking pan and a wooden spoon to pretend cook.
6. Do some of the prep work early (e.g., when child is napping) so it takes less time away from the child later in the day when she can be a bit more fussy or needy.

HOW TO STAY AWAY FROM (OR BREAK OUT OF) A "FOOD RUT"

We've all heard, at some point, parents say things like, *"I serve the same foods to little James just about every day. He eats yogurt, cheese, and fruit for lunch every day. I do it because I know he'll eat it. If I take time to prepare something new, I'm just not sure if he'll eat it or not."*

We have all been there, and we completely understand! The last thing you want to do is take precious time (and as a parent, we know your time is precious!) to prepare something only to find that your little one refuses to eat it. But if your child is regularly exposed to different foods, flavors, and textures on a daily basis, he will be much more accepting of the novelty! It will be the norm rather than the exception.

We have found that the key to creating a good eater is exposing your child to new textures, flavors, foods, and colors as early as possible. Our mission in creating this cookbook was, and still is, to develop wholesome, family-friendly recipes designed to promote a well-rounded eater right from the get-go.

Sometimes, no matter how hard you try, you may find yourself in a food rut. This usually happens around the 12- or 15-month mark. We've both been guilty of food ruts with our kids, on a number of occasions. Amy's son loves peanut butter and jelly sandwiches. They are easy for Amy to prepare, he looks forward to eating them, and she knows he'll eat them! So she began serving them to him frequently for lunch. Too frequently, perhaps, because when she tried to serve something new for lunch on occasion, she was met with resistance. *"No, no fish. Peanut butter and jelly!"* her son would exclaim.

On the other end of the spectrum, serving the same foods over and over again may result in "taste fatigue" for some children, where the child becomes tired of eating that same food over and over. If you find yourself in a food rut with your child, know that it is a common problem. Here are a few tips to help you and your little one break out of the rut!

1. DON'T DENY CHILDREN THEIR FAVORITE FOOD. Taking their number-one choice away completely will only cause upset for both you and your baby. If your toddler of 15 months seems to want to eat only yogurt and fruit, allow him to continue eating it—just not at every meal. Try saving it as an afternoon snack, or serve it a few times a week versus every single day. Make it something that he can look forward to.

2. DON'T MAKE YOUR CHILD'S FAVORITE FOOD THE DEFAULT. If you try to serve your toddler a food and she refuses it, and then you pull out the old standby food of what she likes, she'll catch on in no time and refuse everything but her favorite. (You know how smart she is!) She'll bank on the fact that you're going to eventually

switch and feed her old faithful, so beware of doing that too much. Remember, it's OK if babies miss a meal here and there. If you have any serious concerns, discuss them with your pediatrician.

3. USE THE "THREE CHOICES" RULE. Provide a three-sectioned plate consisting of three foods in small quantities to start. Make sure at least one food is something that you know your toddler will eat and enjoy. For example, if you know your toddler loves strawberries, place a few bite-size pieces of strawberries in one section on the plate and two other options, such as chicken and broccoli, in the other compartments. Your toddler may dive in and go straight for the strawberries, and that's OK! If she asks for more strawberries without touching the other two foods, encourage her to at least try the chicken and broccoli first.

TROUBLESHOOTING PROTEIN

It's pretty common for even the best little eaters to suddenly reach a phase where they suddenly want nothing to do with meat protein, such as chicken, fish, or beef. This often occurs around 15 months of age. Luckily, we have some tips that can help you and your child through this "meat fickle" phase:

- POUND IT OUT. And we don't mean with fist bumps (although do those too, if you find they work!). Take a rolling pin or meat mallet and pound the meat so that it's thin and flat, no more than one-quarter-inch to one-half-inch thick. If your baby or toddler gets a thick, tall piece of meat in her mouth, it might deter her during this phase. Let her slowly readjust to the texture and consistency of meat by serving her thin pieces that are easy to handle. Once she takes a bite of meat and doesn't spit it out, pound it out with fist bumps to celebrate!

- BREAD IT. Once in a while, you can try serving the meat breaded. Try our *Dance Party Chicken Nuggets* recipe in this instance! The result is delicious, and it adds an interesting, crispy texture that your child may find pleasing during this phase.

- IMMERSE IT IN A DELICIOUS SAUCE. Bite-size pieces of meat swimming in a delicious tomato sauce, for example, is often positively received! Two prime examples are Chicken Tikka Masala and Chicken Parmesan. The sweetness of the tomato sauce is often very appealing to babies and toddlers, and a sauce doesn't make the meat seem like "the main event."

- SLOW COOK. Many parents swear by slow-cooked meals because the food is easy to prepare, delicious, and the whole family enjoys it, including their kids! What omnivore wouldn't enjoy meat so tender, it falls right off the bone? Try our *Slow Cooker Chicken Tacos* recipe for a meal the whole family can enjoy!

- SERVE IT SMALL, BOTH IN SIZE AND QUANTITY. When you serve meat to your child, cut it into pieces that are very small—slightly smaller than she's used to. Getting large chunks of meat in her mouth may seem distasteful during this phase. Think small in terms of quantity too. Start by placing only two or three small pieces of meat on her plate with the rest of her meal. Small quantities may help her feel less overwhelmed.

- DIP IT. Toddlers love to dip! Serve the meat with a dollop of your child's favorite dipping sauce, such as yogurt (regular or Greek), hummus, sour cream, mashed avocado, honey mustard, or ketchup. Show him how to poke the meat using a fork and then dip it into the sauce. Now that he's involved, it makes his overall dining experience interactive, interesting, and more fun!

The good news is that for most kids, "meat fickleness" is just a phase. If you're really concerned, talk to your pediatrician. If all else fails, there are plenty of other high-protein foods you can turn to in the meantime, such as eggs, lentils, beans, Greek yogurt, cottage cheese, or peanut butter. Try our *Poached Eggs, Warm Lentil Soup with Cumin and Coriander, Bean Salad,* and *Tempeh Fingers with Easy Tzatziki* recipes during this phase.

PROFESSIONAL BIOGRAPHIES OF
DOCTORS AND SPECIALISTS

JuliSu DiMucci-Ward, RD, CDE

JuliSu DiMucci-Ward is a registered dietitian (RD), certified diabetes educator (CDE), and a specialist in pediatric nutrition. She graduated with a master of public health from the University of North Carolina–Chapel Hill in 1989 and a bachelor of science in community nutrition from the University of California–Davis in 1984. She has worked as a pediatric feeding educator, nutritionist, and diabetes educator at Spartanburg Regional Healthcare System and a pediatric dietician at Greenville Memorial Hospital in South Carolina. Additionally, she is a professor of nutrition at the Edward Via College of Osteopathic Medicine. When JuliSu is not working, she enjoys hiking, scouting, walking her dogs, cooking, and reading. She's married to wonderful man, David, and is a mother to three active boys, ages 13, 20, and 24.

Dee Harris, RDN, LDN, CDE, IFM-CP

Dee Harris is a registered, licensed, and certified dietitian and nutritionist and a certified diabetes educator. She is also a certified functional medicine practitioner through the Institute for Functional Medicine. She is the owner of D-Signed Nutrition, LLC, in Bonita Springs, Florida. She previously worked with best-selling author, speaker, and researcher Dr. David Perlmutter at the Perlmutter Health Center. There, she customized diets for patients with neurological, gastric, and hormonal issues, including autism, epilepsy, and ADHD. She continues to use food as medicine to treat multiple medical imbalances and disorders by individualizing each patient's plan and supporting lifestyle changes. Dee graduated from the University of Georgia and completed her dietetic internship at Cornell Medical Center in New York. Dee and her husband live in southwest Florida. They have two grown, married children and love to visit their twin baby granddaughters in Charlotte, North Carolina.

Elissa Levine, MD

Dr. Elissa Levine graduated from Princeton University before attending Boston University School of Medicine. She completed her pediatric residency at Jackson Memorial Hospital in Miami, Florida, in 2001. She received additional training in respiratory and developmental pediatrics in New Zealand before settling in Charlotte in 2003. Dr. Levine currently practices pediatrics and is a nutrition and outdoor enthusiast. She, her husband, and their two daughters enjoy hiking, camping, gardening, and taking care of their pet chickens.

Lindsey McKeon, RD, LDN, MA

Lindsey McKeon is a registered and licensed dietitian with over ten years of experience. Lindsey is passionate about healthy living and helping individuals find a balanced lifestyle. She devotes a considerable amount of time to working with clients who have eating disorders, disorder eaters, weight management, and diabetes. Lindsey has two little girls and a loving husband whom she encourages with all her professional advice; however, she admits, "they sometimes are my toughest battles!"

Stephanie Mottola, ND

Stephanie Mottola is a naturopathic doctor (ND) whose practice focuses on supporting the body's natural ability to heal and be well. A cornerstone of unobstructed wellness is a diet including a diverse array of minimally processed plant and animal foods.

Dr. Mottola earned her naturopathic doctorate degree from the National College of Natural Medicine, the oldest nationally accredited naturopathic medical school in North America. She continues her education as a healer studying plant medicine in the Piedmont and mountains of western North Carolina and working with clients in her private wellness practice in Charlotte. She also enjoys hosting food parties with her partner, John, her dog, Etta, writing, dancing, freestyling, playful sarcasm, laughter, bike commuting, and yoga.

Maya Shetreat-Klein, MD

Maya Shetreat-Klein, MD, is an integrative pediatric neurologist, an herbalist, an urban farmer, a naturalist, and author of *The Dirt Cure: Growing Healthy Kids with Food Straight from Soil* (Simon and Schuster, 2016). Dr. Shetreat-Klein completed the University of Arizona's two-year fellowship in integrative medicine and subsequently wrote the Introduction to Integrative Neurology curriculum. Dr. Shetreat-Klein has lectured nationally and internationally for both physicians and laypeople on such topics as children's health, education and time in nature, botanical medicine, biodiversity, and the relationship between our health and the natural world. She has testified on topics such as fracking, safe products for children, and the impact of chemical exposures on children's health. She practices in New York City, where she teaches about terrain medicine.

Stacey Vanderwel, RD/LDN

Stacey Vanderwel, RD/LDN, is a registered dietitian. She received her bachelor's degree at Texas Woman's University in Denton, Texas, and successfully completed her dietetic internship at Patton State Hospital in Southern California. She began her career at Children's Medical Center in Dallas, Texas. This is where she began the love of pediatric nutrition and eventually met her husband, Mark. She is currently in private practice in Charlotte, North Carolina, where she enjoys educating families on how to feed their families in a healthy, balanced way, incorporating all foods into their lives. She has three children, Fana (9), Lucy (7), and Bos (3). She enjoys yoga and cooking.